EVERY-DAY LIVING

Memories of a Family from Blaine, North Carolina

— DOUG RUSSELL —

TABLE OF CONTENTS

PROLOGUE

This book started out as just "a drive around the old places," as Uncle Bill Russell put it, one winter's day. During that drive, Uncle Bill was wonderfully detailed in his memories and stories. He was insightful and funny. Almost eighty years old, he seemed much younger. My favorite photo of him as a child is below.

Uncle Bill's Superman shirt (cool!)
(Courtesy of Bill Russell)

During the course of researching and interviewing, several reasons for writing this book emerged.

First, after spending thirty plus years in engineering management in Austin, Texas and Phoenix, Arizona and a few other places, I wanted to reengage with my extended family from North Carolina. I wanted all of my extended North Carolina family to know that—while I may now sound funny to their ears—after all these years I am still one of them in my heart. More so than I realized.

Second, there are many small towns in America that are disappearing or have disappeared, just like the once vibrant Blaine and Eldorado communities in this book have essentially disappeared. JD Vance talks about this process so clearly in his superb book, *Hillbilly Elegy*. I wanted to explore how this touched my family's communities.

Third, each of our three kids has said at one time or another something like, "Who are we, Dad? Who are our relatives? We see them once every few years, but who are they as people?" Two of our kids go to school in California, where a huge "red/blue" cultural gulf makes people from North Carolina seem like aliens. As one son remarked, "Dad, people from North Carolina aren't like the people out here think they are. Our family are nice people."

Yep. I always thought so.

Along those lines, this book is meant as a sort of family oral history, gathering and writing down family connections to interesting subjects like gold mining, as well as character-revealing and interesting stories of Cled and Lola Russell's—my dad's parents—family from Blaine, North Carolina. In some small way, I hope that my kids will see a little bit of themselves in some of their relatives, and will grow to know their people as people doing "just every-day living," as Uncle Bill once described it.

Finally, I wanted to spend some time with the last remaining Russell sibling who had lived in Blaine, Bill Russell. I wanted people to see the world of Blaine back in the 1940's and 1950's when Uncle Bill was growing up. Through his eyes.

He agreed to show me around the area where they grew up. The map at the end of this section shows the places we are going to visit. Amazingly, the entire route is no more than about fifteen total miles.

Many hours were spent gazing at microfilmed copies of old deeds, some from the 1830's. Deeds were handwritten well into the late 1800's, making some words illegible. Occasionally, the edge of a page was not microfilmed, so context could be lost. The descriptions of where the land being described actually *was* located, can be confusing, and mistakes could have been made. So, a word of caution. Any mistakes are mine, and, if reported to my Goodreads author page, will be corrected in a future edition. Or you can call Uncle Bill. He'll get the word to me!

Finally, while doing research for this book, I universally received stony, "Has Doug lost it?" looks when I mentioned the subject of my "new book." I haven't lost anything. To the contrary, I have found something precious and wonderful in reconnecting with my people and their stories. I hope you enjoy them as much as I do!

Everyone loves a story about hunting for gold and gold mines. That's where we're going to start. At a family gold mine. Or two.

Legend:

✝ Church

◄ 1. Blaine house

2. Hicks house

3. Eldorado house

4. Hopkins house

⚒ Mine

Low Water Bridge

⬤★ Baseball Field

✕ Tannery

✝ Graveyard

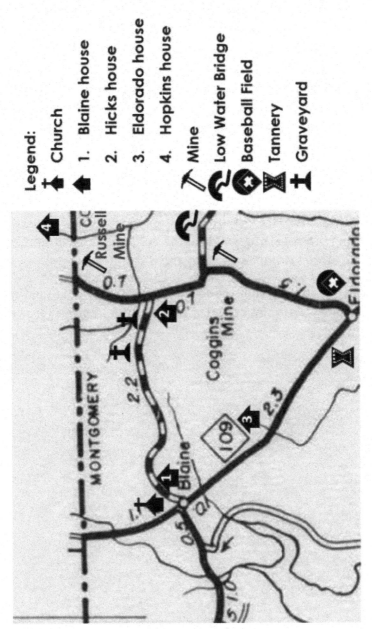

Route around Blaine
(Annotated by Anne Russell)

CHAPTER 1

Russell Gold Mine

Uncle Bill Russell is showing me where my father's family grew up. We reach the east end of Center Church Road. Uncle Bill turns left onto Coggins Mine Road. He drives a mile or so, almost to the Randolph County line. He waves an arm towards a nearby hill.

> Bill: "Russell Mine is right up at the top of that hill to the right. What's left of it; Russell Gold Mine. We'll go by there in a minute."

> I'm stunned. Uncle Bill is talking as if nothing is in the least odd. But, previous to this conversation I had never heard of a Russell Gold Mine. In his whole long life, my Dad, who talked about his family and Blaine, North Carolina a lot, never once mentioned in my hearing that we had a gold mine in our family's past. And my sister, Brenda, had no memory of the mine, either.

When I said something to Bill, I assumed there wasn't much to it. As you'll see, I was wrong.

> Me: "I didn't know there was such a thing. I've heard there was a *Coggins* Mine."

> Bill: "Oh, yeah. Used to play in the Russell mine. There is an open cut down there…"

Me: "Actual gold come out of there?"

Bill: "Oh yeah! And there's a hole down there. The diameter is probably thirty or forty feet. I'd say it is seventy-five feet deep."

The Big Cut (NC Geological Bulletin #3, 1896)

Later research revealed that Bill is describing the Big Cut, shown above. Here's an excerpt about the Big Cut from "Gold Mining in the Uwharries," by Kenneth W. Robinson, published in the Fall, 2008 issue of the Tar Heel Junior Historical Association:

> *"The huge pit covers about an acre. Its walls reach much higher than some trees now growing in the bottom of the mine. Near the bottom of the pit, large tunnels extend sideways into the walls. A separate vertical shaft also was excavated near the open pit. Workers dug quartz rock containing gold from the mine and carted it down the hill to a stamp*

mill next to a creek... There, crushers began the process of breaking the rock and getting gold from the ore... Steam engines powered the crushers and separators. Miners had to load rocks and ore into mining carts, operate hoists, keep steam engines stoked with wood, and—once gold was separated from rock—dispose of the rock {called spoil). They did much of the work by hand... The mine operated off and on into the late 1800s..."

Bill: "And then there's a cave in it. There's an old car in there, and skeletons of animals. We used to play in them holes."

The Russell Mine is now entirely within United States Forestry Service land. Access is restricted. No one plays in those caves anymore!

Present Day Entry to the Russell Mine (Author's photo)

Gold in the Piedmont of North Carolina

The first gold discovery in the United States occurred in 1799, less than forty miles west of the Uwharries. A kid named Conrad Reed found a 17-lb nugget on the farm of his father, John Reed. John Reed used the nugget as a doorstop for many years before finally selling it to a jeweler for $3.50. Eventually John got on the ball and started a gold mine of his own. Reed's Gold Mine—a tourist attraction now— was the result.

Gold was so prevalent in North Carolina from 1804 to 1828 that *all* domestic gold coined by the United States came from the state. The value of gold mined in North Carolina from 1790 to 1860 has been estimated at $60,000,000.

So, as far as Montgomery County goes, in 1825, about fifteen miles from Cabarrus County's eastern border, Matthias Barringer noticed an exposed quartz vein oriented perpendicular to the bed of Long Creek. As he dug into the vein, he struck a much richer deposit, or "nest", and continued to follow the vein. His trench was ultimately thirty to forty feet long and up to fifteen feet deep. For these efforts, Barringer collected more than 750 troy (31.25 grams vs. 28.45 grams for avoirdupois or standard) ounces of gold. Deposits by various Barringers to the Philadelphia assay office were noted in our searches.

By the 1830's, there were at least fifteen mines opened in the area, including the Russell Mine.

Mines were either placer mines, where high pressure water was used to wash gold from a hillside, or they were pit mines. These pits could be shafts or pits dug into the ground. Russell Mine was mostly open pit mines.

**Cradle Rockers at the Russell Mine
(Eldorado Outpost)**

Cradle rockers, shown above, were filled with ore and a bit of water, then rocked side to side in an effort to separate the gold from the dirt and other minerals.

An article by Bill Fields, titled "Gold Rush," in the March, 2017 edition of *Pine Straw* magazine, described the mine's working conditions:

> "By the middle of the 19th century Russell Mine was the biggest gold mine in Montgomery County and the subject for a detailed 1853 report from the Perseverance Mining Company projecting millions in revenue over the course of a 60-year lease on the 40 acres of mineral land... Hundreds of people lived near there, in homes and shack. There was a general store and a hotel across the street. Forty-some miners worked on a shift, and they'd run 24 hours...Miners would earn less than a dollar a day for their dirty, exhausting labor... The ore was crushed by 190-pound 'stamps' that fell the height of a man or more, pounding the gold into a fine substance. This equipment allowed a mine to process 20 to 50 tons of material daily instead of just a few tons."

A report from the UNC Department of Earth Sciences says that several factors worked together to "foster an economic and industrial expansion in the agriculturally dominated region." These factors included development of new mining techniques, the establishment of capitalized mining companies (for example, the New Russell Gold Mine), and increased governmental support for the mining industry.

The infusion of cash from all of this activity—and from the Bechtler and Charlotte Mint's gold coins—increased the state and federal money supplies, allowing North Carolina to move away from its nickname as the "The Rip van Winkle" state.

The Russell Mine had numerous pits, vertical shafts, and adits (horizontal passages for the purposes of access or drainage) within belts of rock. There were at least 6 of these belts within a distance of 2,000 feet across the strike, and they were known as the "Little Lead," the "Big Cut," the "Riggins Hill Lead," the "Soliague Lead," the "Walker Lead," and the "Laurel Hill Lead." See the illustration below.

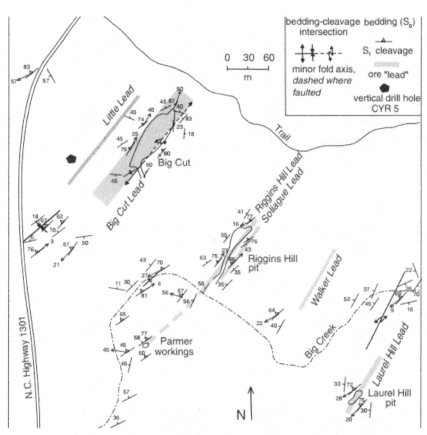

Six Main Workings at Russell Gold Mine
("Russell Gold Mine Deposit, Carolina Slate Belt," 2007)

Russell Gold Mine
(NC Geological Bulletin #3, 1896)

A picture of the Russell Gold Mine from an 1896 geological bulletin is shown above.

There are five tracts of land that have, as a group, been referred to over the years as "The Russell Gold Mine," in one form or another. As such, these tracts could be traced with some accuracy over the years as they moved from one owner to another. When the mine was sold as an entity, these five tracts were often sold together.

The tracts and some of the keywords used to track them follow. "Big Creek," is sort of a super keyword, appearing in all five tracts, so I won't repeat that keyword phrase.

Tract 1: Spring Branch, 60 acres, "T" stone

Tract 2: George Hearne, Pond Branch, Mrs. Coggins line, 48 acres

Tract 3: Meeting House, Green Davis, West Harris, Steed, Mary Harris, 48 acres

Tract 4: Randolph County line, Z Russell's, 185 acres

Tract 5: County line, Richard Beans, Walter Beans, 200 acres

Corporate names used over the years included The New Russell Gold Mine Limited of London, England; the Manteo and Perseverance Mining Company; Peebles Gold Mining Company; and, of course, simply The Russell Gold Mine.

Significant time and effort was spent in tracking the history of ownership of the land of the Russell Gold Mine. Many, many hours were spent combing the excellent records in the Montgomery Registry of Deeds online data base, the Family Search.com and Ancestry.com websites, as well as the North Carolina land grant file. Trips were made to the Atlanta and Philadelphia National Archives, as well as the Charlotte Mint Museum. No lift-able stone was left unturned.

Uncovered in that process was a second extended family gold mine, the Beaverdam Creek gold mine, started by my fourth generation great-grandfather on Grandma Lola's side, Col. West Harris, Jr. Wow!

A state geologic report in 1896 on the Russell and nearby Steel Mines said, "The early history of these two lode mines is obscure. Gold was discovered at the Steel mine about 1832, but no information concerning time of its discovery at the Russell site could be found."

Etheldred Harris (younger brother of Col. West Harris) received land grants from the State of North Carolina in the 1790's. One of them (#536) appears to be at least a portion of tract 3 of the Russell Gold Mine.

A Jesse Harris (cannot identify within family) received a land grant for what turned out to be tract 2 of the Russell Gold Mine. Also, West Harris, Sr. (fifth generation great-grandfather), Col. West Harris, Jr., (his son, already mentioned) and West Harris (probably Col. West Harris' oldest son, West Early Harris) received a total of thirteen land grants in the area between 1783 and 1801.

The July 4, 1826 *Western Carolinian* announced: "...the discovery of Gold on the land of West Harris, Jr. [Colonel West Harris to us], four miles from the narrows on the Yadkin River in Montgomery County..."

Records were found of several Harris' depositing gold at the Philadelphia assay office in 1832 and 1833. These included a Thomas Harris. West Early Harris had a son named Thomas. Reports indicate Eli Harris from our genealogy also had a grandson named Thomas.

Below is a photo of a deposit by "CW and ER Harris" (CW is probably Charles Wesley Harris, but I cannot identify an ER Harris) from North Carolina, on October 18, 1833 at the Philadelphia Assay office.

Deposit-Philadelphia Assay Office (Author's photo)

In 1845, Eli Russell purchased tract 2 from Charles West Harris (great-great grandfather), and parcel 3 from an E.F. Morgan. Eli and his brother Zebedee, often called Zeb, play an important role in the history of the mine.

During the 1840's, a significant portion, possibly all, of the mine was owned by a JM Worth. Individuals with the names J Worth, JM Worth, JA Worth, and Jonathan Worth made deposits of hundreds of ounces of gold at the Philadelphia assay office during the 1840's, presumably from the Russell Mine. One such entry is below. I did no research to see if this Jonathan Worth is the famous Randolph County Jonathan Worth. It seems reasonable.

Eli Russell and James Russell also made deposits during that decade. There are James Russells in our genealogy.

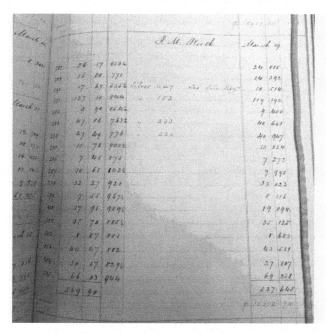

JM Worth deposit at Philadelphia (Author's photo)

In October of 1853, JM Worth sold several tracts of land around Big Creek and near the Randolph County line—likely meaning it was part of the Russell Mine land—to Zebedee Russell. In November of 1853, Eli and Zeb leased and sold land to the Perseverance Mining Company, including the Russell Gold Mine, after which the events of the Tyson Matter, discussed below, occurred.

The Russell Mine got caught up in the "Tyson Matter," an interesting financial dispute, which concerned Henry Tyson of Baltimore, Maryland and Charles F. Fisher of Salisbury, North Carolina. The dispute was covered by a delightfully interesting set of letters, now stored in The Fisher Family papers at the University of North Carolina. Most of the letters were between JH Bryan, and his son, WS Bryan, who were Tyson's two lawyers.

Charles F Fisher   Henry Tyson
(Wikipedia) (B&O Railroad Archives)

The object of the controversy was the sale and ownership of the Manteo and Perseverance Mining companies of North Carolina. Included in the company operations were the Jones and Lafflen gold mines in Randolph County and the Russell gold mine in Montgomery County.

Tyson was from Baltimore, as were the three men who incorporated the Perseverance Gold Mine in North Carolina in 1852. Tyson was elected President of the Perseverance Mining Company in 1853 and served for three years or so. An interesting man, Tyson later served as Master Mechanic for the B&O Railroad, and US Shipping Commissioner in Baltimore.

No less interesting, Charles F Fisher was the CEO of the North Carolina Railroad, and was also a state senator. A Colonel in the Confederate Army, Fisher was killed in the Battle of First Manassas in 1861. Fort Fisher, near Wilmington, was named in his honor.

In June, 1854, Henry Tyson, perhaps growing tired of managing a gold mine, or maybe just trying to cash in on the boom, sold the Perseverance Mining Company (including the Russell Gold Mine) to Charles F Fisher for $75,000.

Fisher gave Tyson two notes for five thousand dollars each, maturing in six and twelve months, and a ten thousand dollar note maturing in eighteen months. Interest was to be charged from the date of the deal. The total was $20,000.

Fisher agreed to pay Tyson any money beyond the $20,000 *only* if Fisher was able to sell the mining property in the future for an amount *over* $20,000.

Nine months later, in March 1855, the termination of a "present lawsuit [was] discussed." After that Tyson wanted to initiate another lawsuit against Fisher, as Tyson alleged that Fisher "obtained an exorbitant price by false and fraudulent representations."

Collection efforts began. On May 23, 1855, Bryan Junior wrote Bryan Senior, reporting that Tyson was "well pleased at the progress made in the collection of the moneys."

Fisher felt the heat. In May of 1856, evidently in an effort to appease, Fisher wrote JH Bryan (the father), that he (Fisher) had not undertaken the purchase on his own behalf or in a manner of specu-lation, but "solely to save what I well knew to be valuable [real] estate from being sacrificed [in a forced sale]."

Fisher then flicked the carrot and the stick. He says "I have expended a large amount of money in the erection of machinery, and in preparing the mines for work, as well as no little time and labor. I had hoped to get for Mr. Tyson Trustee in a short time a considerable payment….most probably this year $50,000. But since hearing from you, [I] have informed the purchaser that I may wish to change the terms to secure immediate payment. He writes of his willingness to be as accommodating as possible...*for a consideration*. If...Tyson requires these obligations to be met at any given Date [sic]...the amount shall be forthcoming... [but it] might be all Mr. Tyson would receive."

In a letter dated May 30, Bryan Junior wrote to his father: "Mr. Tyson was in my office this morning...He says the statements in [Fisher's] letter are not correct...Mr. Tyson and others assure me this contract truly describes the agreement. Some year or two ago, when they importuned Fisher for payment, he very coldly wrote them, that if they chose to sue him, he could delay them for at least three years. They wished Fisher sued to the May/June term, but as they do not know that he is solvent they...are willing to give him a reasonable time to pay...if they get the $16,000 to 17,000 due to them by the notes, they are willing to run their chance for the rest...

Our clients...direct me to caution you [about] trusting...Fisher. They say he is a very subtle man and is exceedingly ingenious in his attempts to get unwary admissions in writing."

In May, 1857 Fisher sent $5000 to Bryan senior for "payment on all of Tyson's notes...I hope to see you before long in Raleigh...We can then have a final and full settlement."

And that seemingly, was that.

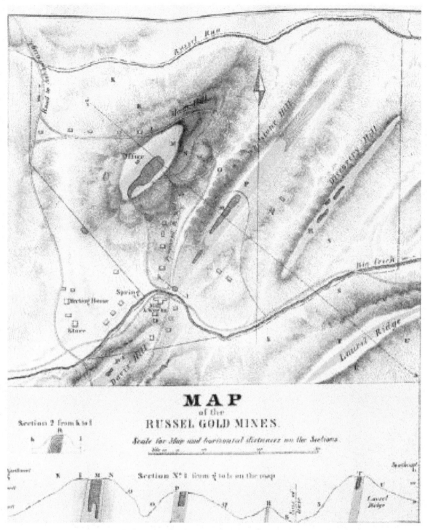

Russell Gold Mine map from Perseverance Gold Mine Days
(Philip Tyson, 1853)

While Charles F Fisher—writing letters, purchasing equipment, sending invoices, and paying bills—was clearly the executive officer in charge for a time, both Eli and Zeb Russell were instrumental in the operation of the mine during that time. Also, a Worth Russell, who I cannot identify within the family, is referenced as working there. John Jehue Russell was one of the early blacksmiths. He was highly valued, as "he could sharpen a drill that would hold its point."

See below for several items from the day-to-day running of the mine. The first photo is a deposit receipt dated September 8, 1855. Eli Russell (in the lower left corner) deposited a gold bar of 18.55 oz., worth $270.33, or about $14.60 per ounce. The line below Eli's entry shows a deposit of 17.13 oz. of amalgam by Fisher.

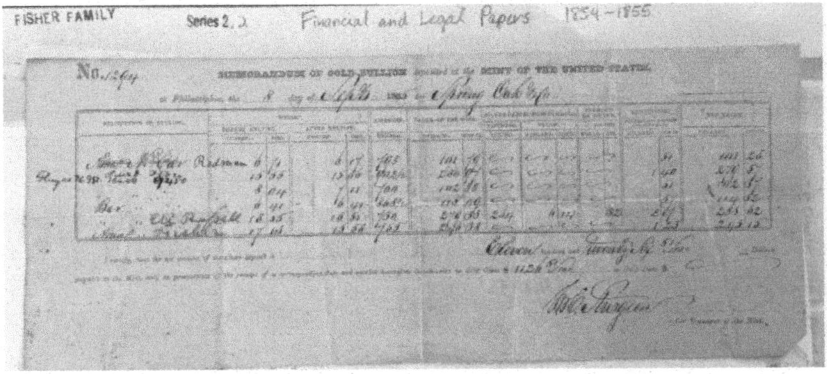

Deposit receipt-Philadelphia Assay Office (UNC Archive)

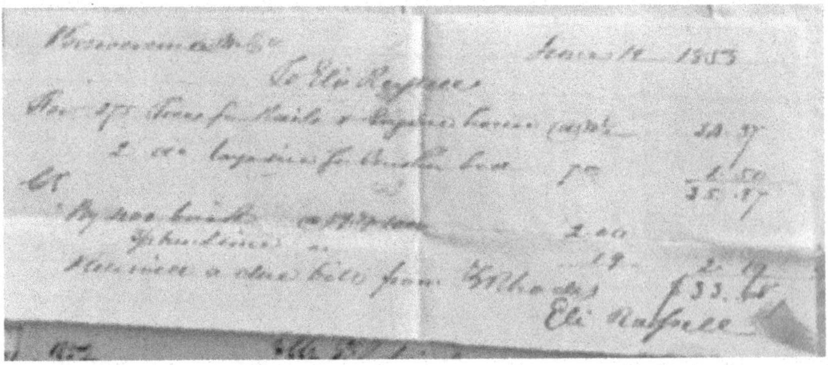

Eli Russell receipt-incidental mine expenses (UNC Archive)

Charles F Fisher became equal partners with a Jonathan Sullivan in the ownership in 1852, as shown below.

Agreement of Fisher and Sullivan partnership, dated November 1, 1852 (UNC archive)

Fisher put the Russell Gold Mine up for sale in 1855 for $25000, as follows.

Agreement to Sell Russell Gold Mine,
September 4, 1855 (UNC archive)

Henry Tyson was commissioned to sell the land in 1855. Records got vague for about 20 years, perhaps because of the Civil War. The land got back to Eli Russell at some point in that time frame.

In 1877 Eli sold the Russell Gold Mine to Peebles Gold Mine Company for $66,000, an amount *worth over $1.5 million now.*

Where that kind of money went within the family is a mystery. By the 1930's the family was dirt poor.

Peebles in turn sold the land to Henry McCoy from Baltimore. In the mid-1880's Henry McCoy and his wife Elizabeth Pinkney McCoy sold land to the New Russell Gold Mine, Limited, a firm based in London, England. In May 1885 Zeb sold 10 acres of land and the right of way through other land to the New Russell Gold Mine, Limited.

Per an 1886 newspaper clipping, BJ Fisher, bought "auriferous [gold bearing] lands adjoining the famous Russell Gold Mine. The transfer was made last week by the administrator of the Zeb Russell estate. The property adjoins the 'Zeb Russell mine,' which is one of the best in the state."

Three applicable deed transactions in this time frame are missing from the online Montgomery Register of Deeds. In 1886, Thomas H Atkins sold Zeb 15 acres near Big Creek.

Luke Soliague, one of six directors of the New Russell Gold Mine, Ltd., moved to North Carolina to act as an on-site agent. One of the six leads on the Russell Gold Mine is named "The Soliague Lead," presumably after him. Line 218 from the Philadelphia Assay office, April 7, 1886 entry page as follows, shows a deposit made by L. Soliague.

Deposit Page-April 7, 1886 Philadelphia Assay Office
(Philadelphia Archive)

In February 1888 the New Russell Gold Mine, Limited, moved its principal place of business to Glenbrook in Montgomery County. In July, 1888 BF Fisher sold a right of way to the New Russell Gold Mine, Limited, for water to be conveyed across his land from the river, "including pipes, drains, or other means."

Seemingly, Zebedee Russell was involved in the operation of the mine right up until the time of his death in 1886. The mine continued to be referred to as the "Zeb Russell Mine" even after his death.

Much more documentation can be found from the later Nelson Russell era at the mine when the mine was called The New Russell Gold Mine, Limited and owned at least part of the time by English investors. Nelson was the third child of seven (only the youngest child was female) of Zebedee Russell and Prudence Hopkins Russell.

A 38-page prospectus for the "North Carolina Gold Mining & Bullion Company," appeared in the June 7, 1891 *"New York Sun"* newspaper. The rather garish top of the first page looks like this:

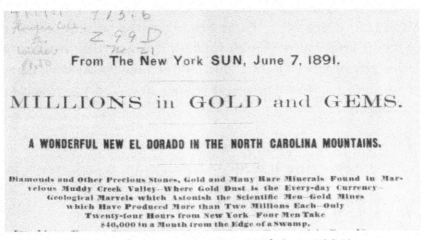

Cover of prospectus (New York Sun, 1891)

The Russell Mine, "New Russell Mine," or "The New Russell Mine Co., Limited," as it was often referred to at that time, was one of the company's investments. Two million dollars in capital was raised at

$10 per share. Included with each purchase was a claim, 25 feet by 100 feet, to be worked by the shareholder. The prospectus claimed that the "company owns nearly every foot of the celebrated Uwharrie River from its source to where it empties into the Yadkin River... There are 22 gold mines in this County....Two of these mines alone have yielded FIVE AND ONE_HALF MILLIONS [sic] DOLLARS IN GOLD (Russell and Copp's Hill)."

There is a lot of this purple prose in the document. For example, "Indeed, there is enough gold hidden in its sands and gravel to build the city of Philadelphia of gold bricks." Sign me up!

Nelson Russell is mentioned several times in the document: "Nelson Russell found a gold nugget weighing eleven pounds, two-thirds of which was pure gold." Later, in an explanation on what the raised capital would be used for: "Nelson Russell's cut is 22 feet deep, and cannot be carried much deeper with the pick without the aid of powder."

And, in a sort of report from the field, the prospectus mentions "One mile and a half from the bridge [Barney's Bridge] we come to the Russell mine, owned by an English company, where 70 head of stamps are crushing the ore night and day. A mile below the Russell is the Appalachian [Coggins]...running on full time with 20 stamps."

Finally, in support of investor relations: "Mr. Nelson Russell and James Cotton, Esq., who worked in the mine, are both open for interviews by a representative of the press, or otherwise."

The California millionaire and co-founder of the Union Pacific railroad, Mark Hopkins—according to the Estelle Latta version of his birth—supposedly worked as an engineer at the Russell Mine, learning much of his business skills there. I cannot confirm that from independent sources.

In April, 1892 Leonard M Russell bought at public auction, for $10,252.55, the bankruptcy assets of the New Russell Gold Mine, Limited, including acreage of 356 and 89 1/2 acres.

In April, 1896, The Glen Brook Mining Company (William Braudreth and George Cranford officers) sold The Russell Gold Mining Company of Arizona land tracts of 356 and 89 ½ acres. How ownership passed from Russell hands after this is vague, as several referenced deeds are missing from the Montgomery Register of Deeds microfilm online records.

The US government first bought the land for the Uwharrie National Forest in 1931 during the Great Depression. In 1961, President John F. Kennedy proclaimed... (the) federal lands in Montgomery, Randolph, and Davidson Counties the Uwharrie National Forest.

The Charlotte Mint

In the early 1800's the only mint in the United States was at Philadelphia. At that time, North Carolina was a very remote part of the United States. Miners there—generally poor—had few options. Bandits were all around. So, gold nuggets, grains and dust were often used as monetary materials. This created many problems, especially when dealing with the local merchants or paying the salary of the miners, not to mention the uniformity of the gold, as well as crimes of robbery and burglary. Even if the miner's gold wasn't stolen, they often had to sell their gold and silver at a loss.

To ease this problem, in 1831 Christopher Bechtler, a German immigrant, opened a private mint in Rutherfordton, seventy miles west of Charlotte. The Bechtler mint was a great success.

Christopher Bechtler (unc.edu)

In little more than a decade, Bechtler recorded the minting of $2,241,840 in gold coins, and fluxed an additional $1,384,000 in raw gold. We discovered at least four deposits of gold or "Bechtler coins" at the Philadelphia assay office during the 1830's by Christopher Bechtler himself or another Bechtler employee. A John Bechtler deposited "Bechtler coins" in Philadelphia in 1847.

In their most active period, from August 1836 to May 1838, the Bechtlers minted approximately $770,000 in gold coins. That sum was astronomical for the period. By contrast, North Carolina's entire revenue for 1835 was a mere $71,740. As might be expected, the Bechtler Mint's impact on the region's economy was remarkable, essentially creating a money supply where there had been almost none. Bechtler coins today are quite scarce and, consequently, command high prices when offered for sale.

The success of the Bechtler Mint soon interested the Philadelphia Mint. The desire to compete with Bechtler was certainly an impetus to provide base mints in the South. U.S. Representative Samuel Price Carson of North Carolina, familiar with the previously mentioned problems facing southern gold miners, on several occasions introduced a resolution to secure a U.S. Mint in the mining region of the Carolinas. One of his chief arguments was the hazard and inconvenience of transporting gold from North Carolina to the U.S. Mint in Philadelphia. Carson's bill, however, was long buried in committee. It was not until 1835 that Congress approved construction of branch mints in Charlotte, North Carolina; Dahlonega, Georgia; and New Orleans, Louisiana.

Charlotte Mint operations began on 12/4/1837. The first coins struck were half-eagles ($5), on 3/28/1838. Over 1 million gold 1, 2.5, and 5 dollar coins were struck from 1838-1861 at a face value of $10.1M.

The Charlotte mint was seized by the Confederacy in 1861 and never reopened. After the war, the assay office in Charlotte stayed open until 1913, sending ingots to Philadelphia. Oddly, Thomas Edison sporadically worked in the basement from 1901 to 1903, where he attempted to extract gold from ore using electricity.

Why Was All That Gold Here?

The Carolina Slate Belt (see picture below) contains the most significant gold deposits in the eastern US. Gold enrichment is associated with a narrow zone of quartz veining.

The Carolina Slate Belt is a 10- to 50-km-wide zone of 450 to 600 million-year-old volcanic and sedimentary rocks extending from Georgia to Virginia. The Uwharrie Mountains are smack in the middle of the belt, slightly southwest of Asheboro in the middle of the map.

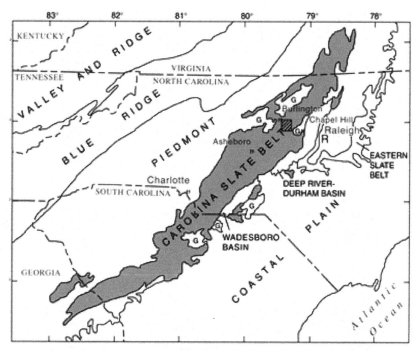

Russell Gold Mine (small black box below Asheboro)
(From rla.unc.edu)

"The Piedmont can be divided into eastern and western areas...The eastern part is the Carolina Slate Belt...and consists mostly of rocks originally deposited on or near the earth's surface by volcanic eruption and sedimentation (North Carolina Geological Survey, 1985). This area is referred to as the Carolina Slate Belt because low-grade metamorphism has given many of the rocks a slaty cleavage.

...The Carolina Slate Belt contains two rock suites: the Uwharrie Mountains contain rocks referred to as either the Uwharrie suite or the Albemarle suite; the Virgilina suite comprises the rest of the Carolina Slate Belt outside of the Uwharrie Mountains. Both suites probably began to form while the Carolina Slate Belt **was near South America** and continued to develop as the terrane moved across the *intervening ocean basin to North America."* (Chapter 2, The Carolina Slate Belt, www.rla.unc.edu, John JW Rogers.)

"Ore grades [at the Russell mine] averaged about 3.4 grams per ton of ore...An evaluation in 1990 of the Russell and Coggins properties identified reserves of 3.6 million tons of ore with an average grade of 1.75 grams of gold per ton of ore." (The Russell Gold Deposit: Carolina Slate Belt, North Carolina report of the US Geologic Survey (2007).)

Do the math. That amounts to the potential of 222,000 ounces of gold still in the ground at the Russell and Coggins mines.

The following might be getting down into the weeds a bit, but I find it interesting. Chemical analysis of the Russell site shows that the highest gold values were associated with the highest arsenic levels. The 2007 US Geologic survey mentions that, "some sort of concentrated arsenic-rich micro-sized bacteria may have been involved," and, "it is possible the gold was concentrated by subaqueous hot springs or deposited on the sea floor in pyrite formations." The theory that the Uwharries moved inland by the floating process called isostasy may account for how this happened.

Where Did the Russell Mine Gold Go?

The previously cited US Geological Service report (2007) says 470 kg., which is about 16600 ounces—over 1000 pounds—came from the Russell Mine. Those numbers are almost certainly low, as they don't cover the gold sent to England or to other sites. The report, which is often cited for the amount of gold mined, wrongly states the mine opened in 1888, which does not account for the previous fifty years of operation.

While our review of the Charlotte Mint records at Atlanta turned up no deposits recorded at the Charlotte assay office during the 1830-1857 time frame from the Russell Gold Mine or under the name "Perseverance Gold Mine," we saw previously that quite a large amount of gold went to Philadelphia during those years. It is possible that Charlotte deposits were made by individuals unknown to us as representatives of the mine.

We did find twelve instances of deposits from the late 1880's and early 1890's for Russell Gold Mine or New Russell Gold Mine at the Charlotte Mint assay office records stored at the Atlanta National Archive. One such entry is shown below. The Russell mine is the fourth entry, 49.48 ounces of gold having been deposited on that day.

		[illegible]	"	6 09
			S.C.	49 88
		Cabarrus	N.C.	5 28
Russell	mine	Montgomery	"	49 48
Ray	"	Mecklenburg	"	4 25
		Union	S.C.	5 81

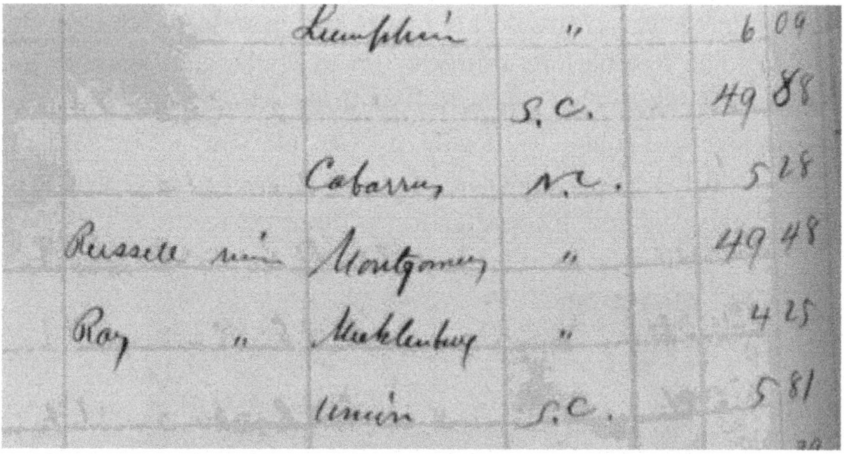

Gold deposit page (Atlanta National Archive)

Finally, records at the Philadelphia office show several deposits from the 80's and 90's. One such deposit, from GW Russell, is shown below, for 1881 or 1887.

Gold Deposit register page (Philadelphia National Archive)

There was a local assay office in Blaine (picture follows). It is possible some gold was recorded at that office. Maybe from there the gold went to the private Bechtler mint in Rutherfordton, or to the Philadelphia or Charlotte mints, or on to England, as some of the Nelson Russell era gold seems to have done. Also, up to the time of the discovery of gold in California in 1848, there was a large demand for Carolina gold by jewelers on account of its beauty, possibly due to its low silver content. It's speculation without the records.

Blaine Assay Office (Author's photo)

Much gold is known to have been exported directly by companies having headquarters abroad, and at least one corporate entity (The New Russell Gold Mine, Limited) was British. Undoubtedly some of the Russell gold went to England.

The Russell Gold Mine was followed with great interest in England's money markets. *The Money Market Review*, a British newspaper similar to our *Wall Street Journal*, was a fifty pages plus weekly compendium of all investing news. Remember, back then they probably got no other financial news, so this newspaper was avidly awaited. There was no MSNBC or Bloomberg back then!

The first highlight below is from the stock quotes tables. I expect the first price is "the bid," or what the dealer would pay for the stock, and the second is "the ask," or what a retail customer would have to pay. The prices are in shillings and pence. Second was the "Advise Gratis" column, where stock advice was given. Such blatant boosting of a stock would not be allowed in the modern financial press. Third, is a periodic "report from the field." The one I have included came from Luke Soliague of the New Russell Mine, Ltd. The entire clipping file is over twenty pages, so space restrictions limit what can be printed. Makes for interesting reading. Really!

Stock quote from 8/11/1888 (The Money Market Review)

**Example of investment advice column from 9/18/1886
(The Money Market Review)**

**11/10/1888 Report from the field by Luke Soliague
(The Money Market Review)**

That's a pretty comprehensive report on the Russell Gold Mine. I had no idea when I started my research just how much there is out there about the mine. There's not quite so much information available about Blaine, North Carolina, which is what we will explore in the next chapter.

CHAPTER 2

Where in Blue Blazes is Blaine, North Carolina?

Well, gold mines are fun, but let's move on and take a look at the place where that and so much else happened, Blaine, North Carolina.

Uncle Bill estimates that there were fifteen or so families, with fifty or more total family members, in Blaine during the years of the 1940's and 1950's in which he grew up. Over the years, people left for jobs and life elsewhere. During our two-hour drive we saw one person. During the course of the research for this book, I found only a few homes in area records.

The online "NC Town Locator" says Blaine is a "populated place" located within Eldorado, North Carolina, which itself is a township of Montgomery County. Alas, no population is recorded, even for Eldorado. Neither place has their own zip code.

Blaine *is* on Google Maps, shown at the crossroad of NC Route 109 and Blaine Road (which turns into Center Church Road or Center Methodist Church Road within our Blaine triangle). With rare exception, the stories in this book all happened within a rough triangle formed by Center Church Road to the north, Coggins Mine Road to the east, and NC Route 109 to the west, with a perimeter of about six miles. For my purposes, I will define Blaine as that triangle, although locals might include a somewhat broader general area.

Driving up to the Russell Mine and to the Hopkins homestead, driving down to Low Water Bridge and back to the main three legs of the Blaine trip adds less than ten more miles to the trip.

To get to Blaine, you drive exactly 69.8 miles east of Charlotte, North Carolina. This puts you in the Uwharrie Mountains. All of Blaine and Eldorado lie within the Uwharrie National Forest. The general perception is that east of Charlotte is sand hills, that is, the way to the beach. What are mountains (tall hills now) doing *east* of Charlotte? After all, Charlotte is in the Piedmont, which means the *foot* of the mountain. And to most people *those* North Carolina Mountains are the Great Smokies or the Blue Ridge, which are in *western* North Carolina.

Turns out that the Uwharries are thought to have once been a coastal mountain chain. Yep, coastal. As in *on* the coast, even though now they are more than 150 miles from the coast. They have gradually moved inland by isostasy—which is a sort of floating—due to the higher buoyancy of the land there versus the previous area. Huh. Even weirder is the theory that the land mass started out in South America.

The Uwharries are estimated to have had peaks as high as 20,000 feet, as recently as 500 million years ago. The highest point is now about 1,100 feet. Erosion, of course. Erosion somehow makes more sense to me than does isostasy. Maybe it is just an easier word on the tongue.

Eldorado as a name for the area—which now seems a somewhat hopeful choice—was absolutely meant with no irony back in the 1800's. As mentioned in the previous chapter, the first gold rush in America happened in North Carolina, and North Carolina was the nation's leading gold producing state in the US until the California Gold Rush started in 1849. In fact, for many years, gold was second only to agriculture in terms of its economic impact to North Carolina.

But to me as a child, Eldorado seemed to have been completely *misnamed*, as the sign "Eldorado" on highway 109 was followed by little more than a country store, empty land, fields, and a few homes. A perfect example of that disappearing-of small-towns thing that JD Vance wrote about in "Hillbilly Elegy."

And from first glance, you might *never* believe that all that follows went on inside one small area and family. As Uncle Billy says, "A whole lot went on around here people don't know about."

So let's get back to finding out what went on! We'll move on to finding out a little bit about the Russells from Blaine, North Carolina.

CHAPTER 3

The Cled and Lola Russell Family from Blaine, NC

Front row: Grandpa Cled, Grandma Lola
Back row: Susie, John Leonard, Madge, Homer,
Devereaux, Agnes, Eugene, Bill
Missing is Dwight. (Courtesy of John Russell)

We'll start with someone with a different last name, Harris. Harris and Russell family members have married some over the years, so you'll see Harris names throughout the book.

*Corilla Safley Harris, "**Ma**" 2/7/1871- 12/17/1953*
Relationship: my great-grandmother on
Grandma Lola's side
Married: Twice
Children: Two daughters. Ethel and Lola (my grandmother).

((◎ ◎))

Great-grandma Corilla Harris was called "Ma" by everyone who knew her. Ma died in 1953, so I never met her. But I sure heard a lot about her.

Ma (Courtesy of Bill Russell)

Great-grandma Corilla Harris was a midwife, as her registration certificate below shows. Below that is a picture of her blood-letter.

After the tool was placed in the desired spot, a line of razor blades on the right side of the tool would pop out—slicing into the target—and "let" blood come out. This was meant to thin the blood. To be helpful, that is…

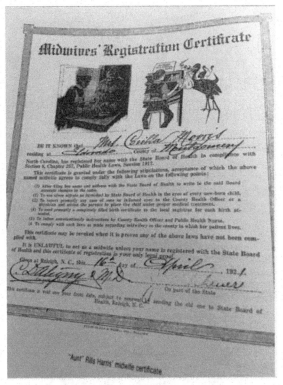

Midwife Certificate (Montgomery Historical Society)

Blood letter (Courtesy of John Russell)

Bill: "So, my Momma's [Lola's] daddy was a Harris. And he died. Went out in the yard after dinner, had a heart attack and died. So then Momma's momma, everybody called her Ma, married Sam Morris. When Ma found out he made liquor she ran him off! Never let him come back!"

Haints happenings

Me: Homer, my dad, had been mightily impressed with Ma's stories about "haints." Haints, near as I could tell, were haunted spirits that interacted with the material world. She believed they existed, and told her stories with such passion that she had a big impact on everyone in the family. They'd better believe! Have you seen her picture? Tough lady.

Eugene's death

Bill: "The night in 1972 before Eugene [Bill's oldest brother] got killed in that car crash; Thursday morning. They had prayer meeting downhill at the church there beside the house. Some of the women would come up here and talk to Momma [Lola] sometimes. Well, she got up that night to see if anybody was going to come up here. They didn't. She was looking out the door and a ball of light come up that old road over there. Come right here, turned around. Then Eugene got killed the next morning." Pause. "Now, about 1:30 in the morning, I woke up to a loud moaning kind of sound. I asked Bobbie, my wife, 'Did you hear that?'

She said, 'I heard nothing.'" Pause.

Bill: "That moaning was the sound he made when he was killed. Popped his neck in a car wreck."

When Ma Died

Bill: "Now." Pause. "An old mockingbird sat on the windowsill pecking on the winder' of her deathbed that day. Its beak was bloody. And Ma died that night on Thursday. And that bird never did peck on that window no more after she died that night." Pause.

Other Haint-ennings

Bill: "The night Susie died, an old music box that hadn't played for years started playing. Explain that."

John Russell (Devereaux' son): "When Mutt [Loy Dennis, Agnes' husband] died, I fell out of my bed. I never fell out of my bed before and haven't done so since."

One more fascinating relative before we get to the Cled and Lola Russell family. Zeb Russell might be my favorite ancestor. He seemingly did it all.

*Zebedee Russell, **"Zeb"** 4/19/1805 - 3/19/1886*
Relationship my great-great-great paternal grandfather.
Married: Prudence Hopkins
Children: Six sons, one daughter.

Zebedee Russell started and ran/worked at the Russell Mine sometime in the 1830s to the early 1850s. The land upon which the mine sat became known as "Zeb Russell's gold mine," even though it was owned by various entities over the years.

Zebedee, along with James L. Gaines, Thomas L. Cotton, Thomas E. Scarborough, Martin Rush, Archibald A. Leach and William Coggins, were appointed commissioners in 1844 to found the Montgomery county seat of Troy "at West's Old field on 50 acres…" Uncle Bill's comment to this news was, "All this time, all those townies thought they were better than us. Wish I'd known *that*."

Zeb was a state legislator from 1846 to 1852, and again from 1854 to 1856, joining Colonel West Harris, Jr. (Revolutionary War, my great-great-great grandfather on Grandma Lola's side) as a close relative who served in that way. Colonel West Harris, Jr. represented the people of Montgomery County in the State House of Commons from November 15, 1792, to January 1, 1793, and in the State Senate in 1797 - 1800, and 1802.

Zeb was listed as a farmer on the 1850, 1860, and 1870 censuses. The 1880 census shows Zeb's occupation as a "dealer in dry goods." It's interesting he never listed his occupation as miner.

I found records that showed Zeb owned many parcels of land over the years. As many other yeoman farmers in the area—who were the majority of landowners—Zeb owned no slaves.

Before secession in May 1865, there was ambivalence in the area's yeoman farmers over fighting what many viewed as the eastern plantation planter's war for slavery. In that pre-secession spirit, the January 23, 1861, edition of the *Raleigh Weekly Standard* documented a pro-union meeting that was held in Montgomery County: "The chairman appointed a committee, consisting of Thos. J. Bright, Zebedee Russell, C.W. Wooley, William Coggins, A. Chambers, Wm. Aumond, and J.T. Buton to draft resolutions expressive of the sentiments of the meeting." Not surprisingly, resolutions came out against secession and decried control by outside interests. J.W. Houston's series of articles in the *Montgomery County Heritage—Volume III* mentions that "70 percent of Montgomery County residents voted against secession in 1861." (p. 82)

After North Carolina seceded on May 20, 1861, Zeb dutifully served in the Confederate Army as a captain, and was pardoned by President Andrew Johnson in 1866. See Chapter 7-Service for a photo of Zeb's pardon.

Prudence Hopkins Russell
(findagrave.com)

Zeb married Prudence Hopkins, from a locally prominent family, who is believed by some locally to be the sister of Mark Hopkins, one of the four founders of the Union Pacific railroad in California. Mark's story is in Chapter 5.

Zeb and Prudence had seven children, one of whom, Nelson, ran the New Russell Mine from the mid 1880's into the early 1890's.

Zeb died on March 19, 1886. Oddly enough, his son Wiley—only forty—died two days before Zeb.

Eli Russell, Zebedee's brother, married Annie Hopkins, a sister of Prudence Hopkins, Zeb's wife. Two brothers in one family marrying two sisters from another family make their children *double first cousins* to each other, the closest relative possible beyond brother or sister.

To make matters even more interesting, Christiana Harris, from Grandma Lola's extended family, married John Calvin Hopkins, Prudence Hopkins' and Annie Hopkins' brother.

Prudence, Zeb, and Eli are buried in the Russell Cemetery, which we will visit in Chapter 5.

***Cled** Russell: 4/15/1890 - 4/15/1973*
Relationship: My paternal grandfather
*Married: Georgia **Lola** Harris*
Children: Nine. Six sons, three daughters

Cled, as a young man (Courtesy of Bill Russell)

Bill: "He'd tell the boys, 'I'll help you one time, then you're on your own.' Let me tell you this. With him having six boys and knowing something about carpentry, he ought to have been a millionaire."

Me: "He was a good carpenter?"

Bill: Vehemently, "Yeah. He was strict about his carpentry. It had to be right."

Me: "How come he didn't do better?"

Bill: "No enthusiasm to work."

Me: "But all *you* boys did. Well, except maybe for John Leonard. Grandpa didn't have enthusiasm for anything?"

Bill: "Now, Homer told me one time that Daddy over there at Blaine raised a bunch of peanuts. Loads of 'em. Wagon loads. And took them to High Point. Couldn't sell 'em! And that just done something to him; he just didn't care no more. Your Daddy told me that."

Me: "Well." Pause. "Why didn't you sell them for him? You got the personality for it!"

Bill: Laugh. "Yeah. I weren't but two or something." Pause. "I went in the tool business. Agnes told that district manager I could sell refrigerators to Eskimos. I don't know about that, but I got a good line of gab."

Bill: "We used to go to the Center Church here. Daddy would sit in the back near the windows that were open. No screens. Set back there, dipping snuff. Needed to spit. Spit right out the window. You could hear him over the preacher." Pause. Laughing.

Bill: "Now. We was in Troy one Saturday in that old '34 Chevrolet. Big old mouthful of snuff. He turned around and spit. His window was up. Spit went all over the winder' and all over everything else!" Louder laugh. Pause.

Bill: "Daddy had the prettiest hand writing. He did script only. Perfect. Only had a third or fourth grade education. Among other jobs, he carried the mail. Back then you had to bid on the route."

Me: "Lowest bid won?"

Bill: "That's right. He'd bring all us kids a Milky Way. Always did that. One Milky Way, we'd have to split it amongst all of us."

Bill: "He was a good and honest man. But a little bit lazy. Didn't want to work too much. He'd work at the shipyard. Make a pot full of money. Come home. Set a while; set on the porch. Spend it. Make more. When he was young, he built houses. There's houses in Eldorado he built. Good carpenter. He would work seven days a week in the ship-yard. I saw some of his check stubs after he died. A feller' name Ken Hall said there wasn't no better man lining up the middle of a ship."

Bill: "Devereaux and Daddy was the nearest thing alike I've ever seen. Even laid out in the casket they looked alike. Devereaux wasn't ever too enthusiastic about working, either. Just like Daddy. Daddy wasn't as 'quire as Devereaux was."

Me: "Grandpa was laid back."

Bill: "Unless you was hittin' on his kids…After Dwight died, Betty Ann [Dwight's wife] was down there at Daddy and Momma's. I was sitting there on the couch. She was downing Dwight. I mean putting him down big time.

And Daddy said, 'Now you hold on there a minute. You just shut your damn mouth. You were just as bad as he was.' Boy, she dropped it and never said another word. Cled *told* her."

Virginia (Devereaux's wife): "All of Cled's kids were independent. They did not let others influence what they did. And they were all hardworking. And honest. They were *all* honest. Billy was the funniest, but Devereaux and some of the others were funny too."

John: "Cled worked at the Coggins Mine, you know. Also, worked on one of the aircraft carriers, either the Hornet or the Wasp."

*Georgia **Lola** Harris Russell Born: 8/17/1897 - 11/11/1982*
The "workingest woman there ever was."
Relationship: My paternal grandmother.
Married: Cled Russell
Children: Nine. Six sons, three daughters

Grandma Lola Russell (r) and her sister Ethel,
who was 2 years younger
(Courtesy of Toni Russell)

Bill: "Now. Me and Devereaux used to tote water to the wash pot and three tubs. Every week. Wore us out. Little 'uns. Once we was worn out, they would move all that down to the spring. Only had to move the water ten feet after that." Laughed ruefully.

Me, incredulous: "Why didn't they just start down at the spring?"

Bill, laughing: "Exactly. That's the thing about it." Pause. Rueful laugh. "That's a fact. Maybe she was teaching us a lesson."

Bill: "Let me tell you this. Momma [Lola] told me that the house in Eldorado [see chapter 8] was Ma's [Corilla's] house. Kept four boarders that worked at the mine. The Coggins Mine. Ma, would go off on a trip to deliver a baby. Sometimes be gone a week. If a woman wasn't able to get up and tend to her family, food and all that, Ma'd stay there and take care of the family."

Me: "They pay her?"

Bill: "Sometimes they'd pay her. Sometimes they'd pay her a quarter, some eggs, a chicken. Or nothing. And she'd go. My momma Lola was 12 or 13 years old. Stayed at Ma's house. Four men staying there at the house. Cookin' for 'em. Washin'. Had an old lard bucket. Fix their dinner [lunch], tote it off all the way to the mine for 'em. Come back. Start supper. Feed 'em. Her about 12, 13 years old. Tough woman."

Bill, about when she was grown: "Workingest woman ever lived in this life. She'd get up of the morning and feed her family, cook biscuits on the old wood stove. At 8:30 she'd go out in the fields. Work for a while. Then eleven o' clock she'd come back in and cook dinner [lunch] for our crowd, nine kids and daddy. 1 o'clock back out to the field. Come back in at four o' clock and feed us again. She had an old washboard. Washed fifty pair of overalls on that thing a week. No help, either." Pause.

Bill: "One time, my dog Tootsie got bit by a copper-head. Right on the lip. Momma fed her a whole mess of hog grease. Tootsie threw it all up and a whole bunch of green poison came up with it. Tootsie was fine the next morning."

Tootsie is on the right! (Courtesy of Bill Russell)

Bill: "Now. She worried about her kids. When any of us would come home after being gone a while—from service, or whatever—no matter how late we got in, she'd hop up and make ham meat and eggs. Didn't matter what time it was, 2AM, whatever. Now, don't you know she laid in that bed many a night worryin'?"

Virginia (Devereaux's wife): "One time John, my son, got really sick. Couldn't keep anything down *or* in. He was four years old. Three trips to the doctor and still wasn't fixed. So I told Lola about it. And she said, 'Well, you probably won't want to hear it, but I can tell you how to fix it.' Well, I was desperate. I don't drink, but I would have tried anything at that point. So I asked her. She said to 'take a little whiskey, set it in a saucer, then set it on fire. It'll burn for a while, but then when all the alcohol is burned off, give him what's left to drink in a little ginger ale or orange juice.' And that worked! I've done the same thing a number of times over the last forty or so years for several people. And it's always worked."

The Nine Children of Cled and Lola Russell

Madge- *9/22/1921 - 12/24/2001*
Married: Hubert Lanier
Children: Clark, Jean, Roger

Madge (Courtesy of John Russell)

Me: "Madge was someone I interacted with rarely. I can't remember five times she spoke to me as an individual. Of course, she *was* the oldest. I remember she got upset, very vocal, at Grandpa Cled's funeral."

Bill: "Yeah. Madge went to pieces when Dwight died. Did something to her. That and her two boys dying."

David Rothrock (Susie's son): "I worked with Roger [Madge's youngest son] for eight years. I liked him. He was a good guy. Didn't seem the type to kill himself."

Bill: "He wouldn't have normally. Roger sat down with a pistol in its holster one time. Accidentally shot himself in the abdomen. Put seven holes in his intestine. His health went down from there. Got a terrible case of shingles on his back. Then he got congestive heart failure. He always told me, 'I ain't going in no rest home.' And he didn't."

Bill: "And Clark. Clark died from a heart attack. In the garage. Workin.' There was no carbon monoxide in his lungs from the car."

David: "Had just prepared himself a glass of tea and his cigarettes were thrown everywhere."

Bill: "Like he had dropped them as he fell."

David: "Yeah." Pause.

●◆●

Me: "So you guys don't have any warm Madge stories for me?"

Bill: "Not really."

David: "No."

Bill: "Well. Here's a *funny* story. Not exactly warm about Madge, I guess. After Momma died, Madge and them started having a Christmas Eve party every year because the family didn't get together no more. Susie just loved it. Lots of people would go down there. You know. It was a way to get everybody together again. Family. Well. It turns out some of them just wanted the get-together to be Madge and her immediate family. And Roger and his wife Linda invited me and my wife Bobbie down there one year without knowing that. It was right awkward. Me and Bobbie never knew why until later."

Eugene: 12/13/1922 – 1/13/1972
Married: Anne Olinger from Blacksburg, VA
Children: Two daughters, Renee and Risee

Eugene as a young man (Courtesy of Bill Russell)

Me: "The only one I was around much was Eugene."

Bill: "Eugene was...flexible. Lively. Wide-open." Pause. "Eugene had a '40 Ford. One Saturday night he was getting ready to go a courtin' in that '40 Ford. Madge and

Agnes and Susie, they didn't want him to go. They set this here road [the driveway from Highway 109 up to the Blaine House where they lived at the time] on fire."

Me: "What?"

Bill: "Yep. It was just weeds back then. The weeds was burnin'."

Me: "What'd Eugene do?"

Bill: "Just drove right through it. Went on about his business."

●◆●

Bill: "Now, Momma always said Eugene's wife was a little bit lazy. Eugene had to do everything. Raise the kids. Everything."

Me: "Dad always said Anne thought she was special."

Bill: "Why was she so special?"

Me: "I'm not sure."

Bill: Nothin' special. I don't know. Eugene just had to do everything."

Me: "He was a good fellow."

Bill: "He was. And he didn't mind doing it, neither."

●◆●

Me: "I miss him. Daddy told me Eugene was going to the University of South Carolina, was married, all at the same time. Getting an engineering degree. That Anne was going to work. As a nurse. Then she wouldn't work. So Eugene had to drop out of college."

Bill: "He was the best person in the world. I don't think your Daddy, Homer, was ever the same after Eugene died. Him and Eugene had two raw pieces of land each over in downtown Winston-Salem at one time. No idea what they'd be worth now."

David: "On Cherry Street."

Bill: "Right."

Me: "Guess they sold them. Dad and Eugene came down to Rock Hill and helped build the Celanese plant. Dad worked there for sixteen years. I don't know how Eugene got from there to Columbia." Shrugs all around.

Brenda (my sister): "Their family used to come up for Sunday lunch and sometimes we would go to their house in Lexington, South Carolina. Mom always fixed roast beef with au jus gravy for him. He loved it. If cantaloupe was in season, she would serve that, too. He always put the beef gravy on the cantaloupe."

Brenda: "Mom also told me one time that Eugene taught her how to make a bed with the bottom corners folded in what was called 'hospital corners.' She used it on our beds. Eugene learned that in the Merchant Marines. And Renee" [his daughter Renee Templeton] "told me that Eugene taught her how to sew when she was a child. He had learned that in the Merchant Marines also."

Virginia: "He worked for Sears. Head maintenance guy, fixed stuff that got sent back. I asked him one time if he enjoyed his job. And he said, 'Absolutely. Love it. Not enough hours in the day.'"

Bill: "Eugene could fix anything."

•◆•

Virginia: "His wife, Anne, was the youngest child. That's why she was a bit spoiled. I found a letter from her parents to Cled and Lola after Eugene's death. The letter mentioned how much they respected and liked Eugene. That was nice."

John: "You know he tested as a genius?"

Me: "No, but I'm not surprised. He was one smart guy."

Virginia: "When he was killed in that car wreck—during that time frame—he was digging his own pool in his backyard? By hand. Now that is some hard worker."

***Agnes**: 5/19/1924 - 12/20/2010*
Married: Loy "Mutt" Dennis
Children: No children

Agnes as a young woman (Courtesy of Toni Russell)

It is an absolute fact in this family that the girls were not as talked about as the boys. That was just a sign of the times. Girls were sheltered back then. They were not allowed to be as "active" as boys.

Agnes was the family scribe and documenter of family historical documents. She was possibly the smartest of a smart bunch of people.

> Bill: "Now Agnes liked to fish. She'd use a straight pin as a hook. Go over to Badin Lake and fish off the Triple C pier. If she didn't catch nothing, it was alright with her."

Bill: "One time she killed a rattlesnake out beside her and Mutt's garage. The garage wasn't connected to the house. You know. She got home before Mutt that night. She stretched that rattlesnake out on the doorstep right where Mutt would step on it."

Me: "Why?"

Bill: "I don't really know."

Homer, my dad. 5/5/1926 - 4/13/2007
Married: *Zelma* Edith Campbell
Children: Brenda and Doug

Homer, as a young boy (l)
Person on right is unknown
Grandpa Cled (possibly) in far background
(Family photo)

Bill: "Your daddy died the same way as the first time I ever seen him. He died the same way as he was when he was a teenager. Same person. He didn't change." Pause. "That I could see. High strung. And level. Honest." Pause. "And he expected you to be the same way with him." Laughter from both of us. "And he was that way when he was young."

●—◆—●

Me: "And he would fight with John Leonard."

Bill: "Yeah. Homer and John Leonard used to fight all the time when they was little. Once Homer got a job plowing a neighbor's fields. He left John Leonard out in the field with our old mule and told him to plow, while Homer went to plow another part. When Homer came back, John Leonard was over under the shade tree, asleep. Homer laid into him good."

Me: Laughing. "Why?"

Bill: Pause. "Well…Homer always was ill tempered. You know. And…John Leonard didn't take no shit. That's just the way it was." Pause. "They was just crossed up." Laughs.

Me: "So did my dad have the worst temper of the boys?"

Bill: "And Dwight. Him and Dwight. "

●—◆—●

Bill: "Daddy brought us a Milky Way candy bar just about every time he came back home after he'd been working somewhere for a while. We'd split it nine ways. And Homer stuttered then. So he said to John Leonard, 'Von eh-eh, Von eh ehh! Coo coo me my kitty car, here come Daddy wid Mikky Way.' Long, loud laugh.

Me: He was saying "John Leonard, John Leonard..."

Bill: "Yeah, yeah. Here it is, 'John Leonard, John Leonard give, give, me my kiddy car, here come Daddy with the Milky Way bar.'" Laughs again. "He stuttered, you know."

Me: "Yeah. Must have heard it a hundred times. That's the first time I ever heard that translated. Never made any sense before. Thank you."

Bill: "When Homer came out of the Army he didn't stutter no more."

David (to me): "Your daddy struck me as kinda' stern."

Me: "Honest as the day is long. But stern is a good word for it. He liked *you*."

David: "Oh, well. I liked him, too."

Me: To David. "You were his kind of kid."

Bill: "I always got along with your daddy."

Me: "You did."

Bill: "I never had no problem with him."

Thomas (Brenda's son): "He had to do an extra credit assignment needed to pass science to finish high school. He told me that was the last year they only had 11 grades in North Carolina; I think this was 1942 since he was 16.

I'm not sure what type of science they were studying or why he was failing, but the teacher let him do an extra credit paper on Thomas Edison. That meant he had to stay after school to use the school library and so he missed the bus ride home. He had to walk home. I'm not sure if this was just one day or multiple days, but he wrote the paper and passed science. I think that is why he and Grannie [Zelma] bought two sets of encyclopedias [Britannia and World Book]. He talked about the advantages the kids who lived in town had over the kids in the country, since the townies could use the library whenever they wanted and easily walk home. He and Grannie wanted to make sure that you and Brenda didn't have to worry about that."

Virginia: "Douglas, your Daddy was interested in history, wasn't he?"

Me: "Yep, all he read was non-fiction. He enjoyed Carl Sandburg's biography of Lincoln. Had a copy of William Styron's *The Confessions of Nat Turner*. He would always say to me, 'Doug, why you reading that science fiction? There ain't nothing real in there.' I can't think of one fiction book he ever read."

Anne (my wife): "*Christy*. He read *Christy*."

Me: "I wonder why?"

Anne: "He watched your mom stay up all right reading it, I think. Guess he had to know what was so interesting. And Christy reminded them of where they grew up, I think."

Me: Dad read extensively on politics, World War II, and avidly read newspapers and watched the news three times a day on local television.

Virginia: "Devereaux was the same way. He would only read non-fiction. I remember a conversation Homer and me had in your house. It was about the Vietnam War. I say it was a conversation, but I said hardly anything. Homer was just telling me about it, not cramming anything down my throat. I'll never forget that conversation about the Vietnam War."

John: "Doug, your dad would give me books to read when I saw him. I still got all the books. Read them, too, in case he asked me about them!"

John: "One time, up at a get together at Grandpa's, Homer invited me to come down to your house to 'bust a few caps.' I was all ready to go hunting with him. But he was talking about drinking a few beers."

His third cousin, Jennie Russell Clark, remembers Homer fondly: "We were best friends all through high school. We lived close to Homer and them. Every Saturday night Homer, John Leonard, cousin Alvin Russell, and Benton Carpenter would all come over to our house and listen to the Grand Ole' Opry on the radio. They were here a lot of other times too."

Class of 1943, Troy High School
Homer and Jennie have lightning bolts over their heads
Andy Griffith's first wife, Barbara Edwards, is two people
to the right of "Mr. T"
(Courtesy of Jennie Russell Clark)

Jennie: "My daddy didn't let us ride bikes. So Homer and John Leonard would bring their bikes down and we learned to ride. When daddy wasn't around, of course." Jennie's dad, Richard Russell—a cousin to Grandfather Cled—who owned 1400 acres and a saw mill, was gone a lot.

Jennie: "Me and Homer were in the same class in high school. When the prom or some other activity like that would come along, Daddy would take me and Homer over to the prom. Homer, you know, didn't have a car at that time."

Jennie: "Homer was fun, nice, and fun to be with. Friendly."

Here are some points about Dad that aren't covered elsewhere.

When I would come home from college, arriving usually in the early afternoon on a Friday, he would sit down and ask me all sorts of questions about the electrical engineering classes I was taking at Clemson University. He was very interested in electrical motors and the mystery of why magnetic fields work the way they do. He always wanted to know why things were the way they were.

Dad was great with his hands and with fixing mechanical things. In fact, he pretty much kept the whole neighborhood's machinery working. If someone had a house maintenance issue, they'd ask him for advice. Usually he'd wind up fixing whatever was messed up for them.

He loved Duke University. The only person in the neighborhood who did. This is when no one liked Duke, before all their basketball success. His love went back to the 1930's and 1940's when Wallace Wade was Duke's coach and took them to the Rose Bowl and other bowls. Dad wouldn't follow the crowd. Duke was a unifying theme for him and me. We made trips to Pauley Pavilion at UCLA and Cameron Indoor Stadium in Durham to watch Duke's basketball team.

Dad coached our church league boys' softball team for three years. Our church was small, and on the wrong side of town. Before he started coaching, the team had always been bad. He would drive around the church vicinity and pick up team members to take them to practice and to games. He was a tremendous influence on the team members. We ran into the best player on the team, our center fielder, in the Western Auto in town many years later and he talked to Dad with real feeling and appreciation. The catcher, a big sad boy with no father at home, came up to us at church one day years later and expressed his admiration and appreciation.

__Zelma__ Edith Campbell Russell, 6/9/1931-10/8/2015
Married: Homer Russell
Children: Two children, Brenda and Doug

Mom at 18 (family photo)

Bill: "Now. We was Looper–clipping. Round piece of material. Clipped off top of socks. ½" wide. Round. From Bisher Hosiery Mill, I think. Looped 'em together. A man would come by and weigh them. Pay us. They're at Wal-Mart now. You can make potholders. We were on porch to the side, working, first time I ever seen Zelma, your Momma. Homer, your Daddy, brought your Momma through there. That was the first time I ever seen her. Prettiest woman on the face of the earth." Pause.

Me: "Y'all liked her."

Bill: "Oh, yeah. I didn't see nothing wrong with her. Always treated us good."

Me: "She was a good person."

Bill: "Yeah. Had a good heart."

Me: "She did."

Pause. Bill: "I remember Cecil [Zelma's younger brother] came down there to your house for a couple of weeks. Didn't Homer put him to work, or told him…"

Me: "Well, it was a disaster. He basically asked him to remove himself."

Bill: "I run up on him, Cecil, when I was in the Army."

Me: "I didn't know that."

Bill: "He was stationed where I was. At Fort Stewart. I believe he was in the MPs."

Me: "He was."

Bill: "He was right across the street."

Me (2), Mom, Brenda (7), at beach
(photo courtesy of Brenda Russell Bonner)

John Leonard 5/24/1928 – 1/23/2017
Married: Marcella Bartlett
Children: One daughter in Europe; One son, Scott.

John Leonard Solo

Me: "John Leonard, Daddy told me, always felt like he got shafted around there. Did he?"

Bill: "Well. He resented the way he was raised. Poor, you know." Long pause. "Mutt and Agnes run that store there in Eldorado. There was some old storehouses out there. And they lived in 'em. About 12:30 one night a woman woke 'em up. She was outside just a squealing. John Leonard and her had gotten into it [fighting] out there in the yard."

Me: Incredulous. "Why?"

Bill: Long look at me. "Who knows?" Nervous laugh.

Me: "Ok." Pause.

Me: I still believe there is something to John Leonard feeling different from the rest of the family. Look at the picture of the Russell kids back at the beginning of this chapter, and the picture below. John Leonard is the only boy wearing a bow tie in the first one. His outfit in the picture below (he's the last person on the right) reminds me of Ernest Hemingway during his Cuban phase.

Family portrait (Courtesy of Bill Russell)
Back row: Devereaux, Susie, Eugene, Madge, Agnes, Bill,
Homer, John Leonard

Couple this with the fact that he attended Appalachian State when he got back from service, then moved to Michigan and worked at GM for 30 plus years, and I am convinced he was the odd pea in the Russell pod.

Bill: "John Leonard borrowed Daddy's old car one night, went to Mutt and Agnes' after he was drunk. Old '34 Chevrolet. Dewey Sanders had a 'tater patch there. John Leonard run all up in that 'tater patch. Then right back on the road. They never did catch him."

Bill: "I mean, he, John Leonard didn't take no shit. They put him in jail one night, in Denton. He'd had a date with a married woman, and he just parked his car out there in front of her house. Had a bottle of liquor sitting in the back. Well, she told on him. And the cops got John Leonard for having whiskey in the car. Put him in jail."

"So two or three weeks later he done something to get back at her. And her and her old man come down there to the Hicks place at about two o' clock, mad, knocking on the door. Daddy got up. Then Momma got up. John Leonard was layin' in there in the bed. They said they wanted to see John Leonard. The woman had just got out of jail. Cause John Leonard had done something to get her put in there. They kept running their mouths. Daddy reached up there above the door, got the shotgun. He brought it down and said 'I want to see you hit the road out there.' Boy, they got their ass out of there."

Me: "I guess they did."

Long pause.

Bill: "They was a whole lot went on around here." Pause.

Bill: "Over there at the Hicks place, John Leonard left in the car, went off drinking. Scared Momma to death. She was afraid he'd hurt himself or kill somebody else. So Dwight and Devereaux went hunting him. They found him, but they couldn't get him back in. So they went to Denton and got the highway patrolman. Kurtman. About 10 o'clock that night, 10:30, here come the car up the old dirt road. Real easy like, with Kurtman right behind him. Kurtman told John Leonard: 'now you go in there and get to bed and behave yourself. I catch you out here again, I'll lock you up.'" Pause.

Bill: "It was rainy and messy. Lord, cold. Dwight and Devereaux just wanted to get him home. Then out in the front yard at the Hicks place, Dwight and John Leonard got to fightin'. You never heard such a scene, such fightin' in your life. John Leonard had accused Dwight of turning him in, of puttin' the patrolman on him." Pause. "It was on, Lord it was on. Blood flyin'; mud flyin'; cold. Lord have mercy. Daddy got up from his bed and said, 'Alright, boys. Break it up.' John Leonard said 'I'll beat your ass too if you come out here.' And Daddy said, 'Well, go on back to fightin' then.' And Daddy went back to bed!" Laughing.

Bill: "Then Momma got her fire poker. That little ol' woman. Couldn't have been much over five foot tall. She got out there and got to bustin' heads. Warpin' frames. They weren't going to hit her. And, Lord, she got to warpin' their frames. Lord have *Mercy*."

Me: "John Leonard would have hit his Daddy?"

Bill: "Yeah, if Daddy [Cled] went out there." Pause. "Drinkin', you know." Pause. "John Leonard, now. He was stout. He'd fight you." Pause. Laughing, "He was…he was one of a kind."

Me: "I didn't know John Leonard. Me and dad [Homer] went to see him up in Michigan in 1987. Dad called ahead, cleared it, set the date, but John Leonard wasn't there when we arrived. We left a note, rented a hotel room in town. Came back the next day, he and his wife Marcella were there. John Leonard claimed Dad had told him it was for the following week. All was well, so we stayed a couple days. His son Scott seemed nice enough."

Bill: "That sounds about right. Here's a story that will show you John Leonard. He wrote home saying he needed $100 wired to him to get him home when his tour of duty was up. Well, he kept the money and re-enlisted. Never told nobody what he done. Momma got to worrying so much that something had happened to him, she contacted the Army. The Red Cross made him write home and explain he was all right. Then, one day, after six years, here come a cab up the drive. John Leonard popped out." Pause. "That was John Leonard."

Me: "My Dad kept a telegram from John Leonard when John Leonard was in San Francisco. He wanted a loan to get home. Dad sent him the money, never got repaid."

Bill: "There you go. That's John Leonard. John Leonard, he was withdrawn. Sat around and wouldn't have much to say. You didn't know what was on his mind. And if you asked him what was on his mind, he would say 'None of your damn business.' And he didn't want to know your business. That's just the way he was."

Virginia: "John Leonard was not as withdrawn as you might think. When John, my son, was in the Gulf War, John Leonard wrote him twice. That meant a lot to John."

John: "Still got the letters."

Interesting story, given that John Leonard was the only one of the nine children to leave the Carolinas, and didn't keep up very much with the rest of the family. I can't remember seeing him more than a couple of times, and never had a solid conversation with him.

Bill: "When he came out of army he went to Appalachian State, was gonna be a lawyer. On the GI Bill. Never finished college. Moved up to Michigan and married Marcella. Worked in Flint for GM his entire working life."

Bill: "John Leonard had a '40 Dodge. Fluid drive. He left it sitting out in the weeds one summer. Weeds as high as the ceiling. He come out one day and started to drive off. Weeds got wrapped around his axle and wheels so tight, he couldn't move no more."

Me: "What'd he do then?"

Bill: "Got out and went back inside the house. Just left it out there."

Me: "What'd y'all do?

Bill: "Pulled it out of there with Homer's Willis Jeep. John Leonard weren't going to do it."

Me: "That just sounds crazy."

Bill: Well?" Long pause for effect. "You didn't know you had a crazy uncle did you?"

Bill: "He played football at Troy High School. [His 1945 team picture is in *Montgomery County Heritage-Vol. III*] I think it was 6 man football then, maybe. I told you about him hurting his shoulder falling off his bike. He was riding in the dark, going fast on a road that had deep ruts. I was scared to drive on it in the daytime, much less at night."

Me: "Yeah."

Bill: "So they wouldn't let him practice like that. Dr. Harris fixed it."

•◆•

Bill: "He'd sleep all day, roam all night like a dog."

Me: "Is that behavior Harris, Russell, or just…"

Long pause.

Bill: "I'm going to say it was a lot of Harris. And some Russell mixed in there."

Me: "Ok." Pause.

Bill: "Russell's got their ways. *Quire-ness.*" [Peculiar] "They're set in their ways." Pause.

David: "Some of the stories Bill told me, if my boys did 'em, I'd put 'em in the nut house. Like when John Leonard and Dwight were driving Grandpa's '47 four-door Ford."

Me: "I haven't heard that one."

David: "Go on." Looks at Bill. "He'll tell you."

Bill: "Dwight and John Leonard were in service. They got home at the same time on the weekend. John was Army; Dwight was in the Marines, so that was always a thing. And they got off one Saturday night and got to drinkin'. Daddy's '47 Ford. Four-door. They took it and went up to Silver Valley. Workers on the road had left mud all over the road, and it rained that night. They went up there to a bootlegger and got some liquor, well, *more* liquor. They got pretty high."

Bill: "They come sailin' through there and hit that dirt and turned that thing over three or four times. Just tore it all to pieces. The top was about that far from the dash. They did that at 7:30. Drove it till 1 or 2 like that. Drove it all over the place. And tore up like that. Sunday morning Daddy got up. Went out and seen that thing." Pause. "It was *on*."

David: "They just came in and went to bed, right?"

Bill: "Yeah." Pause. "That didn't bother them."

Me: "What'd Grandpa do?"

Bill: Laughing. "What? Went and had it fixed. Wrecker come and got it."

David: "Bill said it looked like it was going to fly."

Me: "And they weren't hurt a bit?"

Bill: "Not a bit." Pause. "Now. After that, Daddy never would loan me or Devereaux a car." Pause. "And *we* didn't drink!" Laughter all around.

Susie: 4/16/1930 – 9/25/2007
Married: **Fred** *Rothrock*
Children: Sheri and David

Susie (Courtesy of Jennie Russell Clark)

Bill: "One day Susie was at the sink. Peeling 'taters, I think it was. Just passed out. The knife went flying up in the air and she fell over backwards. Out cold. Never knew what caused it."

"Susie bought me my first caterpillar. You'd wind it up. Had rubber tracks on it. I *played* with that caterpillar. In some ways Susie almost raised me. I was the youngest and she was about the right age. You know."

David: "Momma roomed with an older woman in Thomasville. I think that's how she met Daddy [Fred Rothrock]."

John: "I'll always remember Susie said, 'We didn't know we was poor until somebody told us.'"

Me: "My dad would say that too."

A picture of Sheri, Susie's daughter, is below. I thought she was the cat's meow when I was a kid. She's ill now, and I'd like to remember her as she was.

**Beautiful Sheri in high school
(Courtesy of John Russell)**

***Dwight**: 9/6/1932 - 9/22/1960*
Married: Betty Ann Lanier
Children: Toni, Jackie, Darlene, Sidney

Dwight
(Courtesy of Toni Russell)

Me: "Now Dwight is somebody Daddy never talked about. Never."

Bill: "Yeah. Dwight was different."

Me: "From the start?"

Bill: "Yeah." Long pause.

●◆●

"Now, over at the Hicks place, him and Devereaux would be pitchin' baseball. Dwight played on the high school team. Now Dwight could throw a baseball and it'd look like a bullet. But he never knew where it was going to go. Devereaux would catch. And Daddy would fuss at Dwight all the time. Him and Daddy didn't get along at all. Just cross talk and all that, all the time. Dwight just didn't take none of his crap, you know. He was just that way."

"But, now if somebody was mistreating a woman or a child, he'd be right up in their grills. He was good about that. One time he and Susie were in a shoe store. Some guys were over in the corner telling dirty jokes. He went right up to them and told them to stop. Another time, Maria Morton, who had polio, was riding the school bus. Some fellers starting making fun of how she walked. Dwight told them to stop, and they did."

Carlene Coggins (who grew up nearby): "Dwight drove our school bus some of the time. The road wasn't paved. One time he got stuck in the ditch. He was nice."

Brenda: "One time Dwight moved back in with Grandma and Grandpa Russell. He and his wife Betty Ann had a big fight. I was eight or nine and it was my summer visit. I would spend a week with each set of grandparents every summer. At the same time—the only time they were ever there at the same time as me—Eugene's daughters Renee and Risee were also there. They were a couple of years younger than me. Dwight used to take the three of us to the old country store down in Eldorado in his car."

Me: "What was he like?"

Brenda: "Quiet, joking, friendly. Nice. He'd get us pieces of candy or give us a few cents to get stuff we wanted. I think he did it because he missed his kids. This one time he was joking around with some of the guys standing around the store. Friendly and all. As he walked away one of the guys said something like 'killing gooks,' and the guy laughed." Pause. Shivers. "Dwight was in Korea, you know. And this look came on Dwight's face. It froze all at once into a blank cold mask."

Me: "Like the thousand yard stare soldiers talk about?"

Brenda: "Yes. And without any inflection, Dwight said to the three of us, 'Get in the car.' Well, I knew what that tone of voice and body language meant, from when Daddy would act similarly. Risee wouldn't get in the car, she was being a brat. So, I grabbed her hard and pulled her into the car. He took us back to the house and then went off by himself for a long time."

A later conversation with Dwight's daughter, Toni

Bill: "To your daddy Toni Ann, there weren't nothing like you to him in the world. You was daddy's little girl."

Toni: Smiling slightly, "Momma didn't like that, I'll bet."

Bill: "No."

Toni: "She didn't like that I wasn't a boy."

Bill: "I don't know about that, but I've seen your Daddy play with you and throw you up in the air. You just a laughing and a carrying on."

Me: "Was the '53 Olds Dwight's only car?"

Bill: "He used mine. I had a '57 Oldsmobile 98 Holiday Coupe and he run the shit out of it while I was at work. He wasn't working. Then he went to work for Edward Harris carpentry and bought that '53 Olds. That's what he killed himself in." Chapter 6 deals with Dwight's suicide.

Dwight is shown in the 1950 Troy High School football team picture. Also, Dwight, twelve years old, did the welcome at the commencement from the Eldorado School (grammar school) on May 23, 1944. Nine-year old Devereaux also saw action, hoisting the US flag and doing a talk called "If I Fess Up Like a Man" *(From Montgomery County Heritage Vol III).*

Devereaux - *5/17/1935 - 1/16/2017*
Married: **Virginia** *Varner Russell*
Children: John

Devereaux (Courtesy of John Russell)

Bill: "Me and Devereaux were down at the old Hicks place, down at the springs. Washin'. And Devereaux was bigger than I was. Three years more. And he kept aggravating me. He wouldn't leave me alone. I told him to stop. And I told Momma. He wouldn't do it. I picked up a rock and knocked him in the head with it."

Me: "That work?"

Bill: Flatly, with satisfaction, "Yep. Well, then I went across the creek and up the hill. She was after me. I thought to myself, 'She'll cool off. I'll stay in the woods until she cools off.' And she did. She cooled off." Pause. "Devereaux was petted to death."

Me: "Why?"

Bill: "He was just one of momma and daddy's favorites. Momma said one time she reckoned Devereaux was her *only* boy who didn't drink!"

Me: "You didn't drink."

Bill: "No." Shaking his head. "I'm crazy enough in my head without drinking that stuff."

Me: "You saw too much."

Bill: "That's right. Now John Leonard would soak it on. A drink of liquor would make him plumb crazy."

•◆•

Bill: "One day Devereaux and Gilbert Futrell was stacking lumber at Denton Lumber Company, which Gilbert's daddy, PP—they called him Pearl—Futrell owned. Devereaux and Gilbert Futrell was friends. Devereaux got too hot stacking lumber. He got too hot. You know when you get too hot, your blood boils your brain or whatever?"

Me: "Ok…"

Bill: "He got too hot. And anyway, he never acted the same after that."

Me: "How old was he?"

Bill: "14, 15."

Bill: "Now, Pearl Futrell. I was in Park-In Grill, getting some lunch, with Bobbie my wife. Pearl walked in. Big, fat. Sloppy clothes. Scruffy hat. Torn blue jeans. Bobbie said 'Who is that?' I said, 'Richest man in Davidson County.' Now. Pearl bought the land for Uwharrie Point. You know what that is, don't you?"

Me: "Yep. Expensive club out on Badin Lake. Held the ACC golf tournament there."

Bill: "Right. He bought that land for $23,000. From a boy I used to run around with, Wayne Taylor. Wayne inherited it. Some man in Stanly County left it to Wayne. In a trust. When he got of age, he sold that land. They took way more timber off that land than woulda' paid for it. They was pines on there a hundred foot tall." Whistle. "One and a half, two million dollar homes. And the people that worked in there were not allowed to speak with anybody who lived in there. Unless they was spoken to, you know." Pause. "And that's the straight." Pause.

Bill: "One time Devereaux hit me in the head with a hammer." Pushed hair on his head out of the way. "Look. See that dent?"

Me: "You sure that isn't natural?"

Bill: Glaring. "Huh?"

Me: "Joking. A joke."

Bill: "Oh, yeah."

Virginia added this to the hammer-head story:

"Billy told that story at Devereaux's funeral. But did Bill tell you why Devereaux hit him in the head?"

Me: "No."

Virginia: "I love Billy. But telling that story at Devereaux's funeral hurt me a little. But that's just Billy. He didn't mean no harm. So, according to Devereaux, Billy had locked Devereaux in the barn or something like that, and when Devereaux got out he was mad and hit Billy. With whatever was nearby. The hammer. That's what he always told me."

Bill: "Devereaux never would ask a girl out much. Tall, good looking boy. So I hooked him up once in a while. One time I hooked him up to this pretty ole girl, Fayden, was her name. He'd go see her on Sunday afternoon. Hop in his car and drive over there. Then in the evening, I'd jump in his car and drive back over there to see her. He didn't know. She was dating both of us at the same time. Devereaux didn't know about it. After four or five weeks, she said, 'This is getting a little stressful for me. One of you got to stop courtin' me.' So I said, 'Well, since I been driving Devereaux's car and using his gas, I guess I'll be the one to stop.' And I did."

Bill: "Later I told him if he didn't get serious with Virginia [Devereaux's eventual wife] that I was gonna' go after her." Devereaux and Virginia's son, John Russell, gazed at me with a horrified look, and said, "Billy coulda' been my Daddy. Can you imagine that?" General laughter.

Virginia: "How Devereaux asked me out. Well. It was Christmas time. There was a play coming up at church. Billy and his first wife [they were not married at the time] insisted I go. At the same time, they were pushing Devereaux to ask me out. I was not initially inclined to go. This occurred a couple of times before I agreed."

Virginia: "Devereaux was a quiet man. Didn't talk much. That was just Devereaux. At first that bothered me a little bit. He never told stories about his family. Billy is the one for that. Devereaux never hollered or fussed at me. He was good to me. He was just quiet. I loved him very much."

Virginia: "Devereaux never revealed anything told to him in confidence. More than one time somebody would tell him something, and then later say something about it in front of me. I wouldn't know what they were talking about. They'd be surprised, but when they looked at Devereaux, he just said, 'What did you tell me?' And they would say, 'To say nothing about it.' And he would nod and say, 'That's right.'"

Virginia: "People say Devereaux was tight, you know, with a dollar. But he wasn't. We supported the boys down at Lake Waccamaw near Lumberton for many years. And other things, too."

Virginia: "But, now. Devereaux *was* a perfectionist."

John: "I've seen him work with a piece of wood, make all the cuts, everything, then say 'I don't like that knot and throw it away. And it was gone."

Colton is John and Kathy's son. Granddad Devereaux was Colton's *candy man*. Super Bubble gum.

> Colton: "I could tell a joke and Grandpa would laugh. My Dad, his own son, could tell the same joke, and he'd just look at him."

> John: "With that stone look of his. I could tell from the location and angle of Daddy's pipe if he was mad at me. If he was relaxed, that pipe would be on the right side of his face. As he got hotter at me, it would move to the other side, just like a gauge. Just like clockwork."

> Virginia: "You know, if he was mad at you, he just wouldn't talk to you."

General nods around the table. Many Russells, including me, often hold a grudge for life.

> Virginia: "I asked him why one time. He said, 'I might say something I regret.'"

Truly, still waters run deep.

> Virginia: "He was a patient man. Here's a story on that. I was washing dishes, just cleaning up in the kitchen one time while he was outside mowing the grass. I could see him through the window, you know, while I worked. I'd look up every once in a while, glance towards him. Well, he'd mow a while. Then I'd see him stop, work on the mower. Mow some more. Then, in a few minutes, I'd see him stop and mess with the mower some more. He did that several times until he was done. Never got mad, never yelled at it. Just patient."

Me: "That's not me. My dad either. No Russell I know well is *that* patient."

Virginia: "Devereaux was. And I never heard him curse. He was just laid back. Right, John?"

John: "Cool as a cucumber."

Kathy, to Virginia: "Y'all were the best in-laws a person could ever ask for. Billy was the most vocal. But Devereaux could deliver a line. He had a deadpan delivery."

Virginia: "Devereaux never got rid of anything."

John: "Nothing. Kept every screw, every bolt, scrap of wood."

Me: "Dad was the same way."

Virginia: "They grew up in the Depression."

John: "Now I go through all his stuff. *All* his stuff. A mess. I can't get rid of none of it. Momma has to do it for me. I hear him in my head saying, 'Son, we might need that someday.' And I just can't throw nothing away."

Virginia: "I'm not taking away from Billy or anybody else. But Devereaux was a master craftsman." See pictures below of furniture Devereaux built.

Furniture Hand-Built by Devereaux (Author's photos)

Furniture Hand-Built by Devereaux (Author's photo)

Virginia: "Devereaux had a set way of doing things. Best vacation I ever remember we went on was to Gatlinburg. It just about killed Devereaux, though. He had the place he would want to see each day and that was it. Me and John were more spontaneous. We would see something and say, 'Let's go there!' And we'd be off."

John: "Only time Daddy and me ever had a beer together. That's a great memory."

Virginia: "You know, Devereaux didn't drink."

Me: "Yes."

Billy: *6/11/1938 - still kicking*
*Married: current wife, **Bobbie** Holland*
Children: No children

Homer, Billy, Eugene
(Courtesy of Bill Russell)

**Bill, Dwight, Devereaux
(Courtesy of Bill Russell)**

Uncle Bill Russell on himself

> Bill: "I hate a liar, a dope head, and a drunk." Pause. "I ain't gonna put up with none of 'em." Long pause. "You know one thing about an alky?"

> Me: "Can't trust them?"

> Bill: "That's right. Can't trust 'em. Now you see me today and you see me next month, I'm the same thing. Consistent. All the young 'uns was honest. But different. They was all different."

Looks across the street at a shopping strip.

> "Now Brandon's wife, [Holly], she's got a tanning booth in there. And a clothing store up there. Brandon, that Sheri's boy."

> Me: "Right."

Bill: "One week she sold $18,000 worth of clothes. Had just opened up."

Me: "Clothes? Clothes?"

Bill: "That's right. They work hard. She got three or four people she's hired. And he fixes houses, works for the police department, fire chief over there at the fire department." Pause.

Bill: "Before Holly and Brandon was ever married. One time he wouldn't ride a Ferris wheel with her over at the fair in Lexington. I rode with her. We was standing there in line waiting for the unloading and we got to talk about working to have something in life. And she said 'Well, how long does it take?' I asked, 'What?' She said, 'To get something for yourself.' I said, 'Just be patient and keep your nose to the grindstone. It'll happen.'" Pause. "They got it going today." Pause. "Gotta crawl before you can walk." Long pause.

On Land

Bill: "I had me 26 acres back when me and Bobbie first got married. I sold it. She wanted a house and I didn't think I could do both. Of course, if I'd a known then what I know now, I would have kept it. You know what I'd done?"

Me: "What?"

Bill: "I would have turned it into trailer spaces. I would have rented them trailer spaces. Not the trailers now, the spaces. Kept 'em nice, curbed, that sort of thing. Would have had me a fortune going."

On Marriage

Bill: "So, I got drafted in 1961. Got married to my first wife in 1960. Your daddy was my best man. Homer. He was my best man.

She lost a baby after a couple of months. We borrowed $2000 from your Daddy. She was a good beautician. And I went on and got drafted. Put up that beauty shop over in Asheboro 'fore I went in the service so's my wife at the time would have something to support herself with." Pause. "Wasn't long after I went in the service she had five operators over there."

Me: "Must have been good at it."

Bill: "Best in the state. She'd always wanted to fix hair. She stayed at Susie and Fred's to go to school over there in High Point. It didn't cost her nothing. Drove my car." Pause. "We going to go by that beauty shop. I'm going to take you down there where that shop was."

Long pause.

Bill: "Well, about 15 months later I come home during the day. I was in service. Nobody was home. On the back porch was a bunch of beer cans. And I said 'Oh, something's wrong here.' I went uptown and got her brother-in-law. He was a preacher. I said 'Don't say nothing about this.' Madge had seen me uptown, and told her I was home. See, I was slippin' in. Unannounced. And Madge let the cat out of the bag. She [his first wife] tried to get one of her friends to go to the house and get those beer cans. But I'd already seen them cans. And whenever she got done with work that Saturday night, and got to the house, I said 'Where'd them beer cans come from?' She said, 'What beer cans?' I said, 'The ones that was here on the back porch. You got somebody over here to get 'em out, I reckon.' I was just guessing, you know. So anyway."

"I went on back to camp on Monday like everything was hunky dory. And I come back after the Cuban Crisis on a three-day pass. She didn't know I was coming. So I went down there to her brother-in-law Hal's house. Hal and me went over to Asheboro. He had an old '54 Chevrolet. We hid the car over there on the backstreet. And walked back up to where me and her lived. She was gone. But her car was sitting there. I unlocked the door to the house and went in. Duplex apartment. The girl who lived next door was home."

"I told Hal, 'You stand here at the back door. I'm gonna' slip outside, and when they come up I'll come in behind 'em. You don't let nobody through here. Somebody already told him [Bill's first wife's friend] that if I ever caught him there I'd kill him. I went outside the house and waited and waited. Finally, they come up in the car. I started out to the car. I had a .38. Then they got out of the car. And I had to drop down. There was a shadow from the streetlight. That light was keying on the white parts of my skin. They were within 15 feet of me, but never did see me laying there."

"They went on in the house, and that girl next door told her I was home. They started back out in a hurry. I caught 'em; came right in behind 'em. I put that damn .38 on him. He got down on his knees, beggin', crying like a damn baby, tears running down. I had the gun that far from his nose. He was begging, begging. 'I'll never do it again,' he said. 'I'll never do it again.'"

"Now. I thought 'What's best for old Bill?' And I said, 'Well, the good Lord told me she could have said no.' I stepped to the side, and said, 'Man, get the hell out of here while you still can.' And I went on in. She had locked herself in the bathroom. She came in and sat on the bed. I said, 'Woman, look up here. My God, are you satisfied?' And I got up, cut the light out, locked the front door, and went. I never did go back in there."

"About a month later, I went over to get my clothes and see about the Army reserve meetings. It was one Saturday evening about 5 o'clock. She said, 'You had any supper? Come on in here and I'll fix you some supper.' I wasn't going in there. She handed me my mail. I sat there on the step reading my mail and she come out there beside of me."

"After I got out of service—I had a '62 Chevy when I was in service—she said, 'you ain't gonna take that.' I said, 'Yes I am. You ain't gonna whore around in that no more.'"

●◆●

Bill: "And when I got out of the service, there was a little girl that worked in the first wife's beauty shop. Gosh, she was pretty. I was cuttin' the block there one Friday night. Every time I'd drive by, that little girl'd wave at me. Finally, when we got to the back side, back where it was dark, she slipped up to me and said, 'You don't know me, do you?' And I said, 'Naw. I ain't had the pleasure.' And me and her got together. My ex-wife found out about it and fired her. Why?"

●◆●

Bill: "Now. After I moved down here. I was working out in the yard one day. A car come by. It had three women in it. They went down there to the end of the street, turned around, come back. They started hollerin' stuff. Her [first wife] and two girls." Pause. "I just told Bobbie about that the other night. Women don't like to hear what went on with a feller and another woman."

Me: Quietly. "No."

Bill: Pause. "I done away with that a long time ago."

Me: "What?"

Bill: "Her." Laughter. Pause.

●◆●

Bill: "Now. Years later. I was over at Lexington getting my feet treated. And a woman sat down beside me. We got to talking. She said she lived in Asheboro. I said, 'I used to live in Asheboro. I got an ex-wife down there somewhere.' And she asked, 'Who is it?' And I told her. She said, 'Naw! She fixes my hair.' I said, 'The hell you say!' She said, 'No, really. She fixes my hair.' I said, 'Well, she fixed mine a time or two, too!'" Laughing. "That woman said 'I got a sister lives right beside her. I want you to meet my sister.'"

Bill: "So the next Monday I was back at the foot place, and her sister came with her. She sat on one side, and that woman sat on the other side. She said, 'I never heard such a din down there. That woman [Bill's first wife] come in there, her face beat all to pieces.'

Bill: "I knew he was nothing but a damn drunk. But what could I say. I'd a got myself in trouble [if Bill had attacked either of them]. I was in service. Didn't want to be in jail and be AWOL-ed out. It wasn't worth it."

Virginia: "Billy is the talker in the family, although some of the others could go on too. I could tell when Devereaux didn't agree with one of Billy's statements. I'll say this. Billy would give you the shirt off his back. That's all you need to say."

Next stop is the Center Methodist Church, George III, and a mysterious guy named Christopher Neale.

CHAPTER 4

King George's Land Grant

Center Methodist Church (Author's photo)

The view of the church above is from across Center Church Road. Route 109 is behind the trees to the left of the church. "The House at Blaine," as it was called within the family, had stood behind where I was taking the picture.

Uncle Bill and me walk towards the graveyard behind the church.

Bill: "Who has the land grant?"

Me: "Dunno'. What's it look like?

Bill: It's a land grant."

Me: "I might have it. I'll have to look through Daddy's [Homer's] papers."

Bill: "I'm going to tell you a story on that. My daddy died. Daddy had stuff upstairs in a trunk. Homer had Devereaux go up there and get that land grant and give it to him."

Me: "I should have brought the folder. I think I've got it. I'll look." (I later found the folder, but no land grant was inside.)

Bill: "Hell, that's back in the time of the King of England. [George III, specifically] This down here is part of that." Spreading his arms wide out expansively out across the Center Methodist Church lot, "You see, this all here was part of that five hundred acres."

Me: "Including the church?"

Bill: "Well, yeah. Of course, the church wasn't here then." Pause. "That land grant. I believe that land grant was 17 hundred something, wasn't it?"

Me: "Mighta' been. Yeah. I'll dig it out. Make a copy or whatever. I think I got it."

Bill: "Somebody's got it, 'cause Homer had it."

Doug: "I think I've seen it. Maybe. So I've probably got it."

Bill: "Ok." Changing the subject. "Some of our kinfolk… There are seven foot tall Russells buried in this grave-yard somewhere."

Me: "Matt [my youngest son, 6' 4," a basketball player, and still growing] would like to be seven feet tall."

Bill: Musing. "Huh. And me and your Daddy just tall enough to stand up against a cat's hind end.

Me: "Yeah." We laughed.

Me: "Ah." Pause. "How many acres were on that land grant?"

Bill: "Five hundred acres."

Me: "And every bit of it has been sold now. Actually, I guess I sold the last nine acres of what Dad [Homer] had for Mom's rest home care."

Bill: "Yeah. It's all gone." Pause. "I've read the land grant. Devereaux went up there and got it. He wasn't supposed to. And he gave it to Homer."

I remember hearing about the land grant every so often. I am not sure I ever saw it. I undertook the mission to find the land grant, get it restored, and available to the rest of the family.

Land Grant location (email to sister):

Me: "Do you know where King George's land grant is?"

Brenda: "I have it."

Me: "Ah."

Later phone conversation with Bill:

Me: "Brenda has the land grant."

Bill: "I knew it. Homer shouldn't have had Devereaux do that."

Me: "I'm trying to get it restored and get everybody copies."

Bill: Grumpy. "Ok."

Getting land grant restored (phone conversation):

Me: "Let's find a restorer and get it restored."

Brenda: "I tried back in the 70's. Dad wouldn't let me."

Me: Sigh. "Well, we can do it now, right? I'll split the cost with you."

Brenda: "Ok. I can look into the people at USC [University of South Carolina] again."

Me: "There must be a restorer's association we could find on the internet. If we find one close, we can have it restored and make copies for anyone who wants one. Present a copy to Billy at his 80th birthday party, maybe."

Brenda: "Ok."

A couple of weeks later we met at a restorer's office in Greensboro, North Carolina. Brenda had unfolded the pieces and placed the land grant between two pieces of glass. From the early 1970's until his death Dad had kept the land grant in a file folder. Being stored folded up had left it creased and brown. It had deteriorated badly.

Here is what the land grant looked like before restoration:

Land Grant before Restoration
(Courtesy Brenda Russell Bonner)

The text says (as near as I can tell):

North Carolina No. 143

George the Third, by the Grace of GOD, of Great Britain, France, and Ireland, King, Defender of the Faith, &c. To all whom these Presents shall come, Greeting: KNOW YE, That We, for and in Consideration of the Rent and Duties herein referred, Have Given and Granted, and by these Presents, for Us, Our Heirs and Successors, DO Give and Grant unto Christopher Neale a Tract of Land, containing 500 acres, lying and being in the County of Anson in our Province of North Carolina.

On the No. E. side of Pee Dee River Beginning at a small red oak standing on the South Side of a Branch called the glady fork on a spur of the long mountain and runs thence No. 50 Wt 283 poles to a stake among a 2 White Oaks & 1 Pine Pointers, then N. 40 Et 283 poles to a stake among 1 red oak, 1 sassafras and 2 small B.O. Saplings pointers, then So 50 Et+ 283 poles to a White Oak, then So 40 Wt+ 283 poles to the first station.

Small print at the bottom:

"as by the Plat hereunto annexed Xh appear; together with all Woods, Waters, Mines, Minerals, Hereditaments, and Appurtenances, to the said Land belonging or appertaining (one Half of all Gold and Silver Mines excepted) to hold to him the said Christopher Neale, his Heirs and Assigns, forever, as of our Manor of Ea Greenwich, in our County of Kent, in free and common Soccage, by Fealty only; Yielding and Paying unto us, our Heirs and Successors, forever, the yearly R of FOUR SHILLINGS , Proclamation Money, for every Hundred Acres hereby granted to be paid unto Us, our Heirs, and Successors, on the second Day of February in each year, at such Places in our faid Province as our Governor for the Time Being, with the Advice and Consent of our Council, shall think fit to direct axx appoint. Provided, always, That in Café the said Christopher Neale his, Heirs, and Assigns, shall not, within three Years from xxxx Date hereof, clear and cultivate, according to the Proportion of three Acres for one Hundred; and also, that if a Minute, or Docket, of These our Letters Pxxxnt, shall not be entered in the Office of our Auditor-General, for the Time being, in xxx said Province, within six Months from the Date hereof; that then, and xxxhter of the said Cafes, these our Letters Patent shall be void and of none Effect. TESTIMONY WHEREOF, WE have canfed Seal of said province to be hereunto affixed. Witness our trusty and well-beloved JOSIAH MARTIN, Esq; Captain-General, Governor, and Commander in Chief, in and xxx our said Province, this 22 Day of January in the xnth Years of our Reign, Anno Que Domini, One Thousand Seven Hundred Seventy Three."

So the land grant is indeed from George III, dated 1773. At that time the land was in Anson County. Montgomery County was not created from Anson County until 1779. However, the land grant shows that the land is not deeded to a Russell, but to a Christopher Neale, for four shillings per hundred acres.

Neale received 39 land grants, either as an individual or with others, from 1759 to 1775. As an individual he received a total of 3,450 acres. Six of his land grants were in Anson County, now Montgomery County.

He was a plantation owner in the New Bern area in the eastern part of the state, possibly a judge or a tavern owner, and a very important man at the North Carolina legislature. Neale was not a land owner in the county as of 1779, although John Russel(l) was. Neale is not shown in the census of 1780, although that is no surprise, as he was clearly just a land owner, not a resident.

How a land grant to Christopher Neale got to be such a coveted item in the Russell family is a head scratcher. Maybe this book will unearth someone who has some knowledge of the situation.

We did find one deed with a land description that "starts at a pin on the Neal Tract." Christopher Neale's last name was often listed as "Neal." The land description alluded to "one of eight parcels divided by Simon Coggin for his wife and heirs." Per the 1910 Eldorado Township map, TJ and VJ Coggins had land all around the Center Church and the Glady Fork. However, no connection was found from Neale to a friend or acquaintance of any local Russell, nor was I able to link the sale of the 500 acres by Neale to any owner with the last name Russell.

Where was the Land Grant land?

The land description outlines the property: *"On the No. E. side of Pee Dee River...on the South Side of a Branch called the glady fork on a spur of the long mountain and runs thence No. 50 Wt 283 poles ...then N. 40 Et 283 poles...then So 50 E+ 283 poles to a White Oak, then So 40 W+ 283 poles to the first station."* The Glady Fork is visible. Center Church is close. That's a start. The plot of land described is in the proper general area (see below).

**General Area described in the Land Grant
(Google Maps)**

Now what?

We know we have a square, since all sides are 283 poles in length, and are connected.

One pole is 16.5 feet, i.e., the length of a survey *pole*. 283 poles (the length of each side of the 500 acre square) is thus 4669 feet. The 4669 foot length to a side of the 500 acre square is confirmed by finding the number of square feet in 500 acres (2,178,000), and finding the square root of that number, which winds up being 4667. This is close enough to 4669 for me!

The numbers in the description helped me orient the direction of the acreage's outline. For example, *No. 50 Wt*, is the direction of North, 50 degrees to West, and so forth.

A spur is defined by as "a short, continuous sloping line of higher ground, normally jutting out from the side of a ridge… The ground sloped down in three directions and up in one direction. Contour lines on a map depict a spur with the U or V pointing away from high ground."

The phrase "spur of the long mountain" is the problem. Many, many maps were examined: old maps, new maps, topological maps, county maps, Civil War maps and every other kind of map I could find. No long mountain is shown anywhere close to our target area on any current or past maps we examined. This presents great difficulty in trying to be sure about the exact location of the land grant property.

There is a "Little Long Mountain," ten miles east in the county, near Ophir, but the Glady Fork is nowhere nearby. However, there is hope. Take note of the 600 meter elevation high point slightly to the northeast of the bottom of our squares. It seems reasonable that point could be called "a long mountain."

So, we (my wife, Anne, that is) cut a square from clear plastic transparency film that matched with the scale of a detailed topographic map such that the area within the square matched 500 acres on the map. Then areas south of the Glady Fork were examined that might have legitimately been considered "spurs" of a long mountain, using the term "long mountain" more as a description than as a place.

See below for three likely areas for the land grant land based on various starting points that reasonably may be spurs south of the Glady Fork. I found three; you may see others. In any case, the resultant land grant squares fall reasonably close to one another, such that we can make some conclusions. I eliminated any starting points that would put part of the 500 acres into Randolph County.

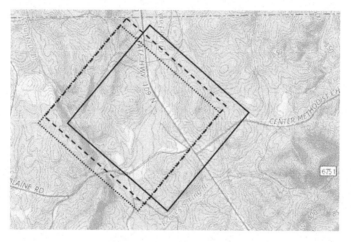

Possible land grant squares
(US Forest Service)

One of the many historical maps that was examined turned out to be a real find. This was a 1910 hand drawn layout by NM Thayer of the Eldorado, North Carolina area, including Blaine and its environs. A section of that map appears below. It is a little hard to read, but still reasonably legible.

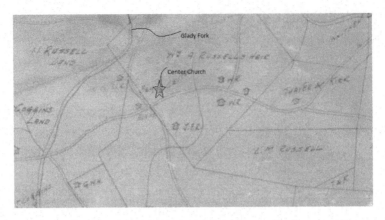

1910 Map of Eldorado, NC (censusfinder.com)

Next, I circled the rough area on the 1910 map that might contain the land grant acreage, as well as any lots of land with the name Russell on them. As you can see, there are many lots associated with Russells in the target area. Up in right corner of the sketch, I also highlighted the Russell Gold Mine.

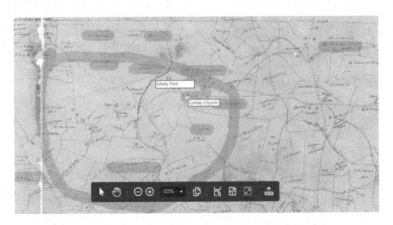

Marked up Land grant area (censusfinder.com)

No story I've uncovered describes any family anecdote about the land grant being passed down across the generations, nor has the name of who in the family might have started with the land. But, nevertheless, I feel comfortable in believing that Russell family members throughout the years owned land in and around the land grant area.

This location also coincides well with Uncle Bill's statements about the land grant being close to the Center United Methodist Church.

This would also explain the obsession Grandpa Cled had for buying land in the target area. At one time he had 100 acres smack dab in the middle of the area, then it had somehow dwindled down to 43 acres by his death, when the land had to be split nine ways for the nine children. Homer, my dad, was able to buy one additonal share of the land, and had 8.38 acres at his death, which has since been sold.

Grandpa Cled's remaining acreage was sold at public auction (see below) to raise cash for the other siblings or their heirs, and has passed from the family.

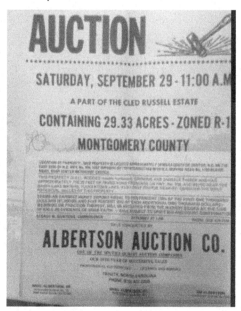

Sad Day (Courtesy of John Russell)

Sad to me, the remaining family members now own none of the original land grant acreage.

During a subsequent discussion with John and Billy

John Russell (Devereaux's son): "Where was the land grant?"

Me: "Brenda has it. Had it since Dad died." (Or so I thought)

John: "I've never seen it. I knew she had it. Never admitted it when we asked."

Billy: "That land grant ought to be with someone else. You or John, someone with the name Russell. I'll tell her that. You want me to tell her?"

Me: Sigh. "No. That might make it worse. Let's just work it."

Later conversation with Brenda

Me: "Why do you want the land grant?"

Brenda: "Because Daddy had it."

Me: "Why did he want it?"

Brenda: "I don't know."

Me: Sigh. "Why was it never restored?"

Brenda: "Back in the seventies I suggested to Dad that we send it to Columbia and have them take a look at it for potential restoration."

Me: Good!"

Brenda: "That ended when Dad said it had to be back home by the end of the day."

Me: "What?"

Brenda: "Dad said the restorer could look at the land grant, it just couldn't spend the night." Pause. "So it couldn't stay there and actually get restored."

Me: "Ah."

After a research trip to Atlanta I stopped by Brenda's house in South Carolina:

Me: "I've got to tell you something. About the land grant."

Brenda: Wary look. "Yes?"

Me: "I don't want you to get side swiped by Bill on this the next time you see him."

Brenda: Intense wary look. "Yessss…?"

Me: "Bill thinks someone else should have it. A male with the last name Russell. That Dad had Devereaux steal it from Grandpa's trunk, and shouldn't have."

Brenda: Silence.

Me: "I personally think it should be with Bill, since he is Dad's last sibling. Bill never said that, I'm just saying if I had it, I would give it to him."

Brenda: "I'm not going to."

Me: Not surprised, and trying not to start an argument, I said, "Ah, well. I understand people might see this issue differently."

Brenda: "After all the things they took out of Grandma's house when she died, I'm not too interested in giving the thing away."

Me: "Me personally, I just want a copy. I don't even really care about having the land grant. And whoever else in the family that wants a copy. Billy, John, David, Scott up in Michigan, Eugene's girls."

Silence.

A later email from Brenda:

"I will send you the flash drive when I get it. Don't worry about the money."

Ah.

Here's what the land grant looks like restored:

Picture of restored land grant
(Courtesy of Brenda Russell Bonner)

The words were easier to read, and the document was one piece of paper. Brenda handed me the hard drive with the files of the land grant images. All seemed well. We complimented Kesha Talbert, who had done the restoration.

Then Kesha asked this question: "Brenda, where had the land grant been?"

Brenda's answer floored me. "It was in a box that Doug returned to me after our mother died a few years ago."

Brenda paid the remaining amount due, we shared some information on our families, and then she and her friend Rick were gone. They didn't even have time for lunch: "Don't want to leave the land grant out in the hot car," Rick said.

"Ah," I said, "Maybe you're right."

So, I guess the joke is on me. Evidently, I had the land grant for the two or so years that Mom lived in Texas with me and my family, and never knew it. When I got home that night, I said to Anne, my wife, "I guess Bill is going to be mad at me now, huh?"

If only Uncle Bill had asked me where it was sooner!

I made copies for Bill and other interested family members.

As I look back on the events around the land grant, the land grant had always seemed an odd thing to covet. A piece of paper. And, after all, it didn't even have our name on it.

I thought of a comment Uncle Bill made about John Leonard, as being "quire," which means odd, or peculiar, in our area of the South. This "quireness" of the Russells from Blaine is often commented on within the family. In fact, my cousin John Russell brought it up independently during a discussion.

John: "Some Russells are just "quire."

Me: "Where's that come from?"

John, shrugging: "You'll go crazy trying to figure out Russells, Doug."

Ok, then. I won't even try.

As Dave Ramsey often says, "Everyone has crazies in their family. If you don't know who the crazy person is in your family, it's probably you!"

In my extended Russell family from Blaine, I *hope* it's not me.

CHAPTER 5

From the House at Blaine to the Hicks Place

Me and Uncle Bill are sitting in his truck at the Center United Methodist Church. We have looked out over the land Bill thought the land grant covered. My cousin, David Rothrock and his sons, Justin and Jordan, are along for the walk and the stories.

Across the road is where the House at Blaine stood.

> Bill: "The Blaine House, the house that my grandfather John F Russell, my father Cled Russell, and all of his nine children except Homer were born in, occupied, and grew up in, is no longer there. The land is now used for horses. Just some memories remain of the Russells there. Carlene Coggins used to own this land. She sold it to a man in Statesville. He's gonna' make a horse farm out of it. For horses that have been mistreated."

> "Carlene's family lived back on an 'ole dirt road there on the other side of Center Church. And they'd walk through our backyard going to the old store. They had a slick path through there, all of them walking." Pause. "She's the only one living in that crowd. And I'm the only one living in this crowd."

Bill and cow in front of barn behind The House at Blaine
(Courtesy of Bill Russell)

As Uncle Bill mentioned above, the house at Blaine is no longer standing. No one even seems to have a picture that is for sure of that house.

> Bill: "Can you imagine? Nine young 'uns in that little ol' house? Let me tell you something. There was a kitchen off to the side, there was a boardwalk. Up here on the porch there was a water bucket. Everybody drunk from the same bucket. Same dipper."

> Bill: "Momma would see a big 'ol mushroom. She'd call that 'the boogerman's snuff.' Scare us to death!" Raucous laugh. "Old mushroom, you know. You'd kick that thang and the dust would just fly. She'd say 'Don't be kicking that! That's boogerman's snuff." Laughs again. Pause.

Bill stops as if he sees something. "Awright. Go up a couple steps right there" Pointing. "And you come into the dining room. Then you come over here to what was called the fire room, where the fireplace was. Called it a fire room. You went through a door here and you went back to where everybody slept back through there. That's all there was."

Me: "How many rooms?"

Bill: "Three. And the kitchen made four. "Yeah." Long, long pause. "But it was a....really rough time."

Me: "Did you know it was rough?"

Bill: "Naw. We didn't know any better." Pause. "I knew everybody. There wasn't many people as poor as we was. That I could see. You know what our Christmas was?"

Me: "No. What?"

Bill: "Passed a box around. Box had oranges, apples, and peanuts in it. Everybody took an orange, an apple, and a handful of peanuts. That was Christmas." Long pause.

Bill looks across the front of the Blaine house lot, down towards Highway 109. "This was all field back then." He points to another area. "Cedars used to be right there. Hell. That old driveway went right up through yonder somewhere. I'm a goin' to try and find it."

Bill: Looking back at David and his boys. "Boys, the driveway went up through there," pointing towards a less treed part of the lot. "We'll have to search for it."

We stomp along for a few minutes.

Bill: "Here's some more buttercups. The house was over there. The road was between the house and the road. We near the house. They's buttercups here. They was all over the place back then."

Justin: After a moment. "This here looks like a road bed. Maybe the driveway."

Bill: Nodding. "Yeah. That's the road bed right there. Come right up beside the house." Excitedly, he walked across the old road and into a clearing. "We're standing in here right where the house was." Waving his hands and looking around. "The old house stood about here, I believe." Pointing to the left: "And the kitchen was right over yonder."

Justin: "There's a bicycle frame over here."

Me: Looking over. "I see it."

Bill: "Weren't mine." Laughs.

David: "Here's a big rock. Kinda' flattened down. And a pile."

Justin: Pointing. "This *here* is all stacked rock."

For several minutes we walked on in silence.

David: "There's rocks all in here."

Bill: Stops and looks around. "I'm looking for a great big ol' tree that stood beside the house."

Justin: Kicking at something. "That looks like something from an old wagon. Leaf spring or something."

Bill: "Yeah. That was probably Daddy's. Or his daddy's." Pause. We walk along.

Bill: "Now we used to come over down here towards the creek. With a mule and a wagon. Daddy had all of the land down in here in corn back then. Good land, not rocky. Near the creek. And I'd sit up here all day long and watch him plow that field with that ol' mule. Under this old shade tree, just bored to death all day long. I was too little to work."

We walk a bit more.

Bill: "Momma'd cook all of the pig, now. Daddy would get her to cook the pig brain with some eggs. He loved that."

Me: "The crackling coming out and all?"

Bill: "Yeah, cooking out the lard."

Me: "Right. Was that called rendering?"

Bill: "Yeah. Rendering the lard. She made cracklins'. I ever tell you boys what the chickens would do when somebody spit out an oyster [mucus]?"

Me: "What? No."

Bill: "All of them chickens would grab at it and pull on it. Stretch it like bubblegum." Loud laughter all around. "I wish that old feller [the current owner] would come around and show us the foundation." Pause. "But I'd bet anything the house was right in here."

We stomp around a while more.

Bill: "I'll tell you. Over here at this ole' house. Didn't have no ceiling in it. You could look through the roof, through the walls. I mean, you know. Rain come through. Wind. You've asked your Daddy about it."

Me: "Yep."

Bill: "He told you the same thing, didn't he?"

Me: "Yep." Pause "Who built it?"

Bill: "I have no idea." Pause.

We walk for a while.

Bill: "Now, I carried water from the spring down yonder. The spring this side of the store." Pause.

"Eugene and Alvin. Alvin Russell, Payne's boy. Run the store down there at Payne's. Down there below where the spring was? Eugene and Alvin used to go down there and fry chicken and stuff. Down there at the spring."

Me: "Yeah."

Bill: "Between the kitchen and the house was a bench. A shelf. That's where you kept a bucket of water. Everybody drank out of the same dipper. If visitors came, they drank out of the dipper." Pauses for effect. "*If* you was thirsty. Whether you dipped snuff, chewed tobaccer,' whatever you done." Pause. "On a cold morning, it'd be froze. You didn't get no water. It was just a crust."

Bill: "Now Momma burned an oil lamp. At night she'd put a postcard in there. Never did catch on fire. A wonder it didn't, ain't it?"

Me: "Yeah. Now why'd she do that?"

Bill: "To knock down the light. She left it on all night, you know." Pause. Looking at the ground. "That right there is where the house stood. I agree with Justin. Right there where's it's sunk in a little bit."

Bill: "There was a big ol' rock side of the house. Ain't there now; can't find it. Once, Momma told Dwight to go out there and move the goat. He put on an old raincoat. He got up on that rock and went to take the chain off. That goat got scared; scared of that old raincoat a flopping around. And that goat moved that rock. He sure did." Pause. "Scared him." Pause.

Bill: "And over there [across the way] is where Carlie and all them would walk across on the way to the store." Pause. "I told you that."

Bill: Looking into the distance. "World War II. Briden. Payne's brother."

Me: "What?"

Bill: "Briden Russell. Blown up on a ship. He lived back over yonder. Was Carlene's uncle." Pause.

Bill: "How it all started: We was settin' in the back yard back down near the shade tree. Listenin' to the old Air Castle radio, when we heard about Pearl Harbor. 1941. We moved to the Hicks place the next year."

Hicks Place

Hick's Place (Author's photo)

We're about half a mile down the road from the site of the Blaine house, driving on the dirt Center Church Road, heading towards the Hicks place.

Bill: Looking out the window to the left. "That over there was Jethro Russell's house."

Me: "Tell me again about Jethro?"

Bill: "Jethro was Daddy's uncle. He was bowlegged. So bowlegged he couldn't hold a 500-pound hog between his knees to save his life." Pause. "Now. He staked logs. And the old horse would get out of the traces. And he'd go around there and get a hold of that horse bridle, shake the horse's head, and say 'Consarned old son of a bitch!' That was his spite word. Consarned. Jethro married Hattie Clodfelter."

Bill: Sotto voce, "That's your kin people."

Me: Reading from my notes, "Jethro worked as a mail carrier, farmer, and saw miller. Son was Hubert."

Bill: "Yeah. Hubert was his son. And Joel."

After about another quarter of a mile, Bill points out his window into a distant field.

Bill: "That boy got killed I was telling you about. Briden. He bought a '38 or '39 Chevrolet. Brand new. Parked it right out there somewhere in that field out there when he went to service [WW II]. Parked it under the shed. He got killed and they never moved it. I reckon it's still setting out there." Pointing. "Right out through yonder."

Me: Wonderingly, as if no was the expected answer. "The car's still out there?"

Bill: "Don't know. Might be. I know people came up there for years and took parts off of it they needed for their own cars."

Me: "Why did his family leave it out there?"

Bill: "They were just that kind of people. Never moved it."

We keep riding along, covering approximately another quarter mile.

Bill: "They've rebuilt this road." Pause. "Now. Me and your Daddy. Homer. Turned that Jeep over. He was driving; I wasn't. He turned that Jeep over. Run it off in the damn ditch." Pause.

Bill: "John Leonard was ridin' that old bicycle home here. He was messing with a rattle in the back. Hit a rut. And he 'toed' it. [Crashed] Dropped his shoulder out of place. And he couldn't ride it home. So he just rolled it while he walked. And he went back to the doctor the next day from school. They put it back in place. Dr. Harris." Pause. "There wasn't nothin' on this road when we lived here." Pause.

Bill: "Now. Down at the Hick's place, you'd never see nobody all week unless you went to church. Well." Pause. "Or unless a load of liquor come through. One time a load of liquor come through, with another car behind it. They was drinkin'. The car—'35 Ford, I think it was—hit the ditch over here. They had the back seat out and had the back stacked full of liquor. They got out. It cut one of 'ems forehead a little bit. And they wanted some water. I went to the spring. Didn't use the family's bucket. Got an old mule bucket that we watered the mule out of and brought it back up there. They drunk out of it. He give me fifty cent. First fifty cents I ever seen in my life. I said, 'Lord, how rich I am.' Later, that old mule would run out over there lickin' the dirt. He couldn't stop himself from licking where that liquor had spilled. Lickin' the dirt, you know." Pause. "Fact." Pause. "Lot of liquor come over this road. Through the years."

Me: "Where would they make it?"

Bill: "I'll show you in a minute." (He never did). Pause. "Over there we used to plant taters." Pointing down at a creek on the side of the road. "Right out yonder is that creek is where we washed Eugene's car in the snow. Big Creek. In my bare feet. No coat on. Just overalls and shirt."

Me: "What possessed you to do that?"

Bill: "Eugene wanted it clean." Pause. "There's an old road. See how big that creek is?"

Me: "Yep." Big Creek meanders up through the Russell Gold Mine land.

Bill: "There's an old fork there that lets you drive right down in there."

Me: "Which car?"

Bill: Pause. "'40 Ford, I believe it was."

Bill stops his truck. We've arrived at the Hicks place, which is only a few hundred feet beyond the Russell Cemetery (shown below). We walk back up to the cemetery. It is on our right as we walk back up the road, a few feet from off the road.

Russell Cemetery (Author's photo)

The Mystery of Mark Hopkins

Me: Looking down at the gravestone of Prudence Hopkins. "Says she died in 1883."

David: "She was 73?"

Me: "71, if I do the math." Pause. Looking at Bill. "They all know the Hopkins story?" Mark Hopkins, he of the Union Pacific Railroad, Promontory Point, Utah, of San Francisco, and great wealth.

Bill: "Yeah. Some of the Hopkins lived right around here. Others was up just over the Randolph County line. You know, back then if you stole a horse, they hung you. So, as the story goes, Moses stole a horse and was also wanted for bigamy, and Mark, his brother protector, had to get him out, and they wound up in California. They didn't strike gold. They traded liquor for gold."

**Mark Hopkins' House on Nob Hill in San Francisco
(Bancroft Library)**

Me: "And he built the Mark Hopkins hotel, or at least somebody did?"

Bill: "And he built a damn railroad. Mark never was married. See Daddy done the history on this. John's got every bit of it. You got to talk with John." [Devereaux's son]

Bill: "Daddy [Cled] did the research on that deal. I hauled him to hell and everywhere. Bobbie [Bill's wife] did too." Pause.

Grandpa Cled amassed extensive genealogy records of the Russell family, as well as the Hopkins family. He did an awesome job with land holdings, and family member connections and lists. I've used some of the information. Alas, I found no verifiable information that tied Mark Hopkins to a North Carolina birth.

As Bill mentions above, family stories abound (dismissed by the New York Hopkins claimees and by California sources) of Mark and Moses Hopkins—brothers of Prudence and Annie— leaving for California so Moses could escape prosecution as a horse thief and a bigamist. Mark then, as the story goes, built a huge financial empire. Moses stole his estate after Mark's somewhat mysterious death. The origination of those stories is not known.

The family Hopkins lived just over the Montgomery County line in Randolph County. Uncle Bill told me how to find the main homestead. Chiggers, snakes, and ticks prevented me from walking back into the woods to actually see it.

There is *no doubt* Zebedee Russell married Prudence Hopkins, or that Eli Russell married Annie Hopkins, from the Hopkins family.

There is *no dispute* that a man named Mark Hopkins was one of the four men responsible for the Union Pacific Railroad, the first transcontinental railroad. Author Richard Rayner, in his book *The Associates* calls Hopkins, Stanford, Huntington, and Crocker "the four men who created California," having "built an empire that controlled one-sixth of the entire US economy."

What *is in dispute* is the original birthplace of the famous man. *The Great American Swindle*, by June Naugle covers both claims, although it is written more like historical fiction rather than a non-fiction recounting of what actually happened. She comes down on the side of a North Carolina Hopkins.

And then there is Estelle Latta. The North Carolina Hopkins birthplace story comes primarily from a book, *The Controversial Mark Hopkins*, by North Carolinian, Estelle Latta. Latta is shown below during one of the many legal battles over the Mark Hopkins estate. Hopkins died intestate—without a will—and his vast fortune, estimated by Wikipedia to be between $20 and $40 million dollars at his death in 1878, was thus exposed to claims. Estelle claimed kinship to Hopkins and tried to reopen his probate in order to get a large portion of the proceeds for her and others.

Two paper slips related to Latta were in Grandpa Cled's files: a receipt for family records from Ruth Lanning, Mrs. Latta's assistant, and a slip of paper with Estelle Latta's then address in Sacramento, California.

Estelle Latta (from newspaper.com)

Mrs. Latta spent 20 years traveling the North Carolina countryside gathering data, telling her story, passing out cold beers, and raising cash to fight the court battle around the reopening of probate of Mark Hopkin's estate. This battle got all the way to the Supreme Court in 1948, with the court refusing to hear it.

POWER OF ATTORNEY

We, the undersigned, are the surviving heirs of MARK HOPKINS, the railroad magnate, whose estate, valued at several million dollars, was wrongfully and fraudulently administered upon in such a manner that we, the rightful heirs, were not given our share of said estate;

We, the undersigned, realize that lengthy litigation is presently taking place in the State of California in an effort to recover Mark Hopkins' estate for the benefit of his lawful heirs. ESTELLE LATTA and RALPH SLATE have heretofore been acting as co-attorneys in fact on our behalf in this matter, pursuant to the power of attorney previously granted to them by the undersigned.

WHEREAS, DR. J. W. SLATE, who had been previously acting as co-attorney in fact with said ESTELLE LATTA and RALPH SLATE, is now deceased; and

WHEREAS, differences of opinion have arisen between said ESTELLE LATTA and RALPH SLATE as to the conduct of the litigation of this matter, —

NOW, THEREFORE, we the undersigned, do hereby constitute and appoint ESTELLE COCHRAN LATTA, FRANK LEE LATTA and ESTELLE MARIE LATTA TUVERSON as our attorneys in fact to carry on the litigation in this matter, in the place and stead of ESTELLE LATTA and RALPH SLATE. Said three co-attorneys in fact shall act together on our behalf. In the event that any of said co-attorneys in fact fails or at any time ceases to be our duly appointed attorney in fact, the remaining co-attorneys in fact or attorney in fact shall continue to act with all the powers given herein as our co-attorneys in fact, or attorney in fact, whichever the case may be.

We, the undersigned, realize that in order to carry on this litigation, it is essential that we act jointly through our attorney in fact.

We, the undersigned, hereby grant said co-attorneys in fact the following powers:

1.   Authorize said co-attorneys in fact by deed, deed of trust, contract of sale, or otherwise, to convey all of our interest as heirs of said Mark Hopkins in order that our consolidated interest or rights may be protected so that a compromise settlement can be made for the group as a whole, as we fully realize that it would be impractical and almost impossible for a compromise to be made individually with each heir.

2.   To represent us in every particular in the investigation, locating, and recovering of the estates both real and personal of the late Mark Hopkins and Moses Hopkins located in the State of California and elsewhere; to have full power and authority to do and perform every act and thing necessary in the above matter as full to all intents and purposes as we might or could do if we were personally present; to institute, investigate, any action that they deem necessary to carry out the purposes above set forth.

**Top portion of Power of Attorney signed by Grandpa Cled
(Courtesy of John Russell)**

Uncle Bill remembers Mrs. Latta coming to the family house in Eldorado. His recollection, "I think Daddy gave her some money a couple of times. I thought it was probably a con then. You know, Momma didn't much like her. Daddy would follow her out to her car every time she came by. She had cold beer out in the car, and Daddy didn't miss out on a cold beer."

In March, 1963 the SEC alleged "that since before July, 1959, the defendant has been making use…of the mails…to offer, sell and deliver securities described as 'investment contracts'…issued in connection with the sale to members of the public of percentage interests in a purported Estate of Mark Hopkins, deceased; and that no registration statement as to such securities has been filed…"

A court ruling in 1965 restrained Mrs. Latta from engaging in acts and practices alleged to constitute violations of the Securities and Exchange Act of 1933. She was charged with the unlawful selling of securities in her efforts to raise cash by putting anyone who contributed onto the heir list, as opposed to ensuring they were rightful heirs. These actions were viewed by the SEC as the unlawful selling of securities. The suit was dismissed in 1971, with her pleading no contest to the findings. She was quite sick at the time and died in 1982.

Mrs. Latta did a great deal of research, but much about her story has been repudiated, and her conclusions themselves are in dispute. She claimed she was a direct descendent of Mark Hopkins. Mrs. Latta's personal genealogy records, used by her with great effect, are in dispute. It is also disputed that she ever graduated from Duke University or attended the University of North Carolina as she claimed in her book. She lived in Durham, North Carolina.

Leaving Mrs. Latta aside for the moment, it is hard for me to understand how someone in our family would concoct out of whole cloth a fictitious pair of Hopkins brothers who disappeared in such a way, with one of them becoming one of the most important men in America. That kind of broad imagination doesn't normally run in our family. Famous novelists like Charles Dickens or the ilk couldn't make up a better story. Mrs. Latta herself does quote Dickens as one of her favorite writers. It is certainly possible she made up the story. I do not know why she would have done that. Perhaps for the attention and money it brought.

Mark Hopkins birth-North Carolina version

As the North Carolina version goes, Mark Hopkins was born on September 3, 1814 in Randolph County, North Carolina. The Hopkins house is just across the Montgomery County line, only a couple of miles from where the Blaine Russells lived. Mark's brother, Moses, who as a bigamist and horse-thief on the run, plays an important role in this story, was supposedly born three years later. No birth records for these two have been reported in any verifiable location in the Carolinas.

This is in no way surprising, as in the 1810's there was no legally required or even standard way for recording births. Claims were made that Mark and Moses births had been recorded in the

Hopkins family Bible. The family Bible was the default standard on the birth and death dates of family members. Such was the case with the Hopkins.

Per Latta, sworn testimony in NC Superior Court from Mrs. Sula Koppelmeyer (whose grandmother was Prudence Hopkins Russell) indicated that Mark Hopkins' name had been in the Hopkins family Bible, and that the Bible had burned up in a fire at Nelson Russell's house. Also, a Blanche Freeman supposedly testified that Mark Hopkins visited the area in 1877, and that she had talked with him, as did others.

Mrs. Latta reported that Mark worked for Zebedee Russell (my great-great-great grandfather) in the Russell gold mine as an engineer. This work in the mine was believed instrumental in the development of the business acumen Hopkins showed later in California.

An indictment for Moses T. Hopkins on grand larceny of a horse is included in Latta's book, but the indictment is not a photo of a real indictment, but rather just typed words. This is hard to understand, as there are photos of other legal documents in her book.

Mark Hopkins birth-New York version

There is clearly more supporting documentation for the claim of a New York birth. *A Sketch of the Life of Mark Hopkins* by Benjamin B. Redding, and *The Associates*, by British author Richard Rayner mention *only* a NY birthplace. The New York Hopkins had a brother named Moses.

To support the New York version, much genealogy research online (See the "Diana, Goddess of the Hunt—for Ancestors!" website mentioned in the bibliography), The California Historical Society itself, and a book by Timothy Hopkins titled *John Hopkins of Cambridge, Massachusetts, 1634, and Some of His Descendants*, all show a New York origin.

Also, author Salvador A. Ramirez has written several books about Hopkins, including a two-volume set over eleven hundred pages long, titled *The Inside Man*, that firmly comes down in the New York camp. Ramirez states in his introduction that repudiating Mrs. Latta was a key reason he wrote the book. Eleven hundred pages is a pretty strong effort at repudiation. I have thumbed through all eleven hundred pages, and they have incredible detail about Hopkins' daily events.

Ramirez also raises the issue that the North Carolina version may have started when Timothy Hopkins, "working to reconstruct his genealogy, placed advertisements in North Carolina newspapers seeking information regarding one of New York Samuel Hopkins' sons and descendants who had emigrated to the state." This may have triggered a young Estelle Latta's imagination.

There is no doubt that there was a Mark Hopkins from New York. Mrs. Latta claimed in her book that there were two Mark Hopkins, one from New York and the real one, from North Carolina. She claims, that, at one time, there were actually three Mark Hopkins in Sacramento.

Conclusion

There are strongly held beliefs within the Russell family that Mark Hopkins grew up near Blaine. There is no independent data that supports the existence of a Mark Hopkins from North Carolina. Most people who might remember anything, even secondhand, are now gone. Uncle Bill helped me find six Hopkins in the Asheboro area phone book. Calls to them furnished no data I could use for the North Carolina side. Only one answered or called me back. If such information comes forward, I will gladly report it in a future edition of this book.

Several questions come to mind, which if confirmed, would support the North Carolina Mark Hopkins theory:

—Can a Mark Hopkins actually be shown to have existed in North Carolina in the right time frame?

—Can a Moses Hopkins, his brother, actually be shown to have existed in North Carolina in the right time frame?

—Can we show that Moses was arraigned in North Carolina for horse stealing and bigamy?

—Can we show that either of these people made it to California?

If the answer to any of these questions is "no," particularly the last one, then the North Carolina Mark Hopkins is unlikely to be the railroad baron Mark Hopkins. If anyone has any information that can help me answer those questions in the affirmative, I hope they come forward.

On a closing note, Mark Hopkins never lived in the house shown earlier. The structure does not exist today, having burned down in the aftermath of the 1906 San Francisco earthquake. And the Mark Hopkins hotel was built after his death.

Mark Hopkins died in Yuma, Arizona on March 29, 1878, under somewhat suspicious circumstances. Hopkins had rheumatism, and the diagnosis was, oddly, "the rheumatism went to his brain."

There you have it.

Mark Hopkins, an enigma to the end. Getting anything close to definitive answers for these and related questions are the subject of another book. I will not delve more deeply into them here.

We walk back to the Hicks place.

Inside the Hicks place, an imminently falling down house (Author's photo)

Bill: "Now. Me and Devereaux used to get off the school bus, go through the house, hit the steps, go to the hog house out back there in the woods. And smoke cigarettes of the evening. Looked like Indians." Pause.

Bill: "Old toilet used to sit right out yonder. This house had electricity when we moved here.

Bill: "Right down yonder, go down behind the house there, that old branch down there, where that walnut tree is. That's where we killed hogs."

Bill: "That room right there, you come out of? That's where Ma [my great-Grandma Corilla Harris, the mid-wife] died. Remember the mockingbird pecking on her window?"

Bill: Pointing through an open window. "See the kitchen in there? Don't it blow your mind? They had a heater in this room. And on the other side of this fireplace, there was another one on the other side."

Bill: "Dwight was sitting up there at Daddy's with his feet on the ottoman. And lighting struck a clothes line down there. Knocked him off of there!"

Bill: Loud. Talking to David's son Justin. "They's an upstairs to this thing, you know!"

Justin: "We *are* upstairs!"

Bill: "Is there anything up there?"

Justin: "No."

Bill: "There used to be a self-playing piano up there." Pause.

Bill: Talking to me again. "Now there was an old cabinet right over there."

"There's where Susie fainted, one day frying fish. She was about 12 or 13 years old. She was standing at that old sink right there. First thing you know, she hit the floor. Never did know why. Unless she was starting her period, or something."

Bill: "They had an old eating table sitting right where you're at. There was a bench, with chairs around it. Mom put a bowl of soup on the table, and some of it would run off 'cause it was unlevel right there."

Pause. "This was a good place to live. Quiet." Pause.

"Now. You talk about making liquor. You could hear 'em cutting wood wayyyy back over in yonder." Motions. "And a way back over in yonder. To fire a still with?"

Justin: "Somebody come in here and ripped off all the boards out of the top."

David: "Who lived here after y'all did?"

Bill: "High-Pocket Cecil."

Me: "I never heard of High-Pocket Cecil." Sounds like an interesting guy!

David: "How long y'all live here?"

Bill: "Moved here in '42 or '43, [when Bill was 5] I reckon it was. Moved to the Eldorado house when I was 18, 19, 20 year old. I'll be eighty in June." Pause. "That's lap siding right over there. And right out there in the yard is where John Leonard and Dwight was fightin' that time."

We walk down the road a ways. We come to an area that Bill describes as what always rumored to be a slave graveyard.

Bill: "When I was here before, nine markers were here. And a headstone for Benjamin Hopkins. He was the slave master, I guess. Hopkins' graveyard, I reckon."

Some sort of site clearing, maybe for construction, had occurred since Bill's last visit, possibly cutting down pine trees, so there wasn't actually much to see. I can find no record that Zeb Russell (or any other close-in Russell) had slaves. Zeb's entry in the 1850 census, says "No" to the question of slaves.

This is not at all unusual. Per the Digital Histories project at the University of Houston:

"In 1860 only 11,000 Southerners, three-quarters of one percent of the white population, owned more than 50 slaves; a mere 2,358 owned as many as 100 slaves. Over half of all slaves lived on plantations with 20 or more slaves and

a quarter lived on plantations with more than 50 slaves. Slave ownership was relatively widespread. One-third of all southern white families [less in Montgomery County] owned slaves, and a majority of white southern families either owned slaves, had owned them, or expected to own them. The average slave owner lived in a log cabin rather than a mansion and was a farmer rather than a planter. The average holding varied between four and six slaves, and most slaveholders possessed no more than five."

Yeoman farmers in and around Montgomery County planted wheat or corn primarily, two crops that, unlike cotton or tobacco, did not require large numbers of field hands. That is the primary reason yeoman farmers in the South owned few or no slaves. There is a mention in Grandpa Cled's records of two slave graveyards in the Blaine area. He does not identify them further.

Me: Nudging a slate marker a few inches on each side, "And now we can only find this one."

Possible slave grave marker (Author's photo)

David: From a few feet away. "But this is weird. Here's a flat rock, here's another one. Seems odd." Long pause.

The Piedmont in North Carolina, including Montgomery County, was certainly no hotbed of abolitionism, but Professor Victoria Bynum lists certain factors that caused many locals to be conflicted by the war. The Montgomery County Historical Society's *Montgomery County Heritage-Vol III* has a similar story (see pages 69 and 70).

First, Piedmont North Carolina (particularly Montgomery County's neighbor to the north, Randolph County) was a strong bed of Whig party Unionism before the war. The Whig party ceased to be relevant during the upcoming Democratic party versus Republican party fight over the issue of slavery.

Second, yeoman (small farms of 200 acres or less), non-slave owning farmers, were in the majority throughout the Piedmont counties of North Carolina. These non-slave owning farmers resented being drawn into the plantation owner's war. "Few...identified...with the wealthy planter class, whose plantations were to the east, near the coast." Quoting one yeoman farmer, "There ain't no account of slaves up here in the west [-ern part of the state], but down in the east part of the state...there's as many [slaves] as in South Carolina...People out here hate the eastern people."

Third, the ethnic diversity of the piedmont settlers encouraged religious and cultural diversity. The Baptist and Methodist faiths had gone through their Great Awakenings. Scottish highlanders and Scotch-Irish brought Presbyterianism. German settlers brought Lutheran, German Reformed, and Moravian church members. The anti-war principled Quakers settled in North Carolina starting in the mid-eighteenth century. They were particularly a force in Randolph County. The egalitarian principles of Quakerism and Wesleyan Methodism caused some in North Carolina to oppose slavery on moral grounds.

None of these factors prevented North Carolina from sending the largest number of soldiers to the war from any southern state, nor did they prevent North Carolina from having the highest casualties of any southern state.

We walk back to our trucks and drive on. We're headed to Low Water Bridge.

Before we go to Low Water Bridge and onward to uncover more funny and interesting stories, I want to cover the disturbing incident of Dwight's suicide, as well as the military service of Cled's boys (and a few other relatives), which are the subjects of the next two chapters.

CHAPTER 6

The Hidden Impact of Dwight's Suicide

This book is meant to educate, inform, and celebrate the lives of the Russell ancestors who lived in Blaine. The darkest story concerns Dwight's suicide.

Dwight shot himself almost fifty-eight years ago, yet I found people's memories *so* vivid that it seemed as if Dwight only left recently. I was only three years old when Dwight died, so I have no memory of him. For me, the events around his suicide have been a mystery shrouded in virtual secrecy. Many people were intimate to the details, as well as intimately wounded by the suicide, yet it was never discussed. At least in my hearing.

Like many folks, most Russells don't readily share emotions. Opinions yes; emotions no. I am going to try to show the impact of Dwight's suicide through their own words and through life events. I'll start with the main drivers that led to his suicide, then share how others in the family—particularly his children—were affected by the suicide and its aftermath.

Questions I asked as I was growing up yielded little information. "What happened to Dwight," I would ask my dad, meaning "Why did he kill himself?"

"Came back from Korea. Had headaches. Wasn't ever right after that," was about all my Dad would ever say.

Dwight was thin and charming. Winsome. Only Devereaux was taller. Photos of him as a young man, as well as many stories within this book, show a sweet, just person. I have been unable to get a feeling of him as a person; the essence of him. When I told Uncle Bill that he said, "Yep. That's Dwight."

Bill: "He went into the Marines at 17, you know."

Me: "Uh, yeah." Long Pause. Thinking, "In the Marines at 17, dead at 28."

Reasons

Bill: "Dwight saw a lot of action in Korea. He didn't tell me much from over there, but he said that once he'd had to sit on a rotting corpse while he ate his dinner."

Me: Wincing. "PTSD, shell shock?"

Bill: "Yeah, they didn't call it that back then. He was in a hospital in California for a while when he got back. Might have gotten into drugs there. After he got back, me and Dwight slept upstairs. He always told me, 'Don't you come in here of a night when I'm asleep without turning the light on.' Nerves all to pieces."

Mental Issues: The Diagnosis

Among Dwight's military records was a diagnosis by the military doctors of *passive dependency reaction*. An article in *Psychology Today* says this about passive dependency:

"Dependent personality disorder is described as a pervasive and excessive need to be taken care of... These individuals tend to be passive and allow other people (often a single other person) to take the initiative and assume responsibility for most major areas... They may be devastated by

separation and loss, and they may go to great lengths, even suffering abuse, to stay in a relationship. Other symptoms include: problems expressing disagreements with others, avoiding personal responsibility, unable to meet ordinary demands of life, easily hurt by criticism or disapproval, willingness to tolerate mistreatment and abuse from others. Complications of this disorder may include depression, alcohol and drug abuse.

Relationship Problems

On a humid day in late May, I met with Dwight's daughter Toni to get her views. Toni is the oldest of Dwight and Betty Ann Lanier Russell's four children. This was the first time in well over forty years that we had seen each other. We met at her daughter Vanessa's house. Uncle Bill arranged the meeting. On the way over, Bill said, "I'm going to tell you. There ain't no telling what she could have made of herself if she'd had a chance."

**Toni, Dwight's oldest child
(Author's photo)**

What struck me was how much Toni Ann resembled Grandma Lola, the "workingest woman in the world," as Billy describes his mother.

Toni showed me the suicide note. The note was written on the back of an envelope from a local business. It read: *"Momma, I'm so fed up that I can't stand it anymore. Now please don't think that I am crazy because I am not. But I love Betty and I can't live without her. So long, Dwight"*

Vanessa: "It was a toxic relationship."

Bill: "I ain't candy coatin' *nothin'*. Just tellin' the truth. He was my brother. Betty Ann was your Grandma. I'm not candy coatin' on either side. They did stuff to aggravate one another. Let me say it like this. If she'd been straight up [not slept around], I believe he would have been straight with her. Once, after Dwight had killed himself, Betty Ann was at Momma and Daddy's. I was on the couch watching. She was cutting on Dwight real bad. Daddy drew up and said, 'Wait a minute, here. Shut your damn mouth. You were as bad as he was.' Nodding. "One was as bad as the other."

Toni: "As the oldest of four kids I can remember Momma and Daddy fighting. I can remember Momma hitting him in the head with a beer bottle. Him laying over one of them heavy armchairs. Bleeding."

Bill: "And one time Dwight shot at her. One foot over her head. Said he wasn't trying to kill her. The law took him to jail. Bond was $3500. Daddy come in there and did some Masonic thing and they dropped the bail to $1500 or something."

Toni: "Once, I was sitting on the floor watching TV with the other kids and coloring. I thought it was Momma and Daddy in the bed. And then Momma busted in the front door. It was Momma's sister that was in the bed with Daddy."

Bill: "My opinion is this: Dwight left Betty Ann and the kids at Camp Lejeune, and then went to Korea. That was a mistake. She'd never been out of Montgomery County, and left alone down at Camp Lejeune like that. She was a real looker, beautiful, and started business on the side with some men, if you know what I mean."

Toni: "Momma wasn't doing right."

Vanessa: "Betty Ann had been sleeping around on Dwight, and he come back with PTSD and…"

Toni: "He come back from Korea with a drug problem."

Bill: "Agnes found a needle on her mantle one time. She had been at work, but he had been in her house, you know. He got that in California. Got his back hurt in Korea. Give him painkillers. He was in a padded cell out there."

Toni told me that Dwight and Betty Ann separated, but never divorced. Even the separation was contentious, as Betty Ann claimed her signature had been forged when she discovered she could get Dwight's life insurance money if they had still been married when Dwight killed himself.

Toni showed me two letters from her mother to Dwight. Both letters were posted in Baltimore, Maryland. Keep in mind that Dwight killed himself on September 22, 1960.

The first letter was dated February 13, 1960. Here are some excerpts:

It starts with, "Well, well so my husband doesn't want me to get a divorce. Well if you think I care you are crazy. I don't need a divorce so go to hell. I know one thing, you can stop writing [my sister]…I now weigh 120 pounds and your little girl [Toni] is doing real good in school. Toni makes real good marks on all her classes…This is the way I see things. I don't need you or any man. By the way when you get out of service I may live with you just to show you how mean I can be, but you will never run over me again."

The second letter is dated June 27, 1960. In the interim Dwight evidently agreed to a divorce. The tone is completely different.

"Dwight as far as I know now our divorce will go through within 30 days…I also wanted to say I really think you are the greatest for taking so much, including the children. And sending them so much money. Don't worry, I know that's how much you loved them all along…Also tell you Mama not to worry about the children for I will take the best of care of them. The children send their love."

> Bill: "One time when Betty Anne was up in Baltimore with the kids, Dwight borrowed $45 from Payne at his store, and went up there. Eugene and Homer found out about that and paid Payne out of their pockets. Just the kind of fellers they were."

> Me: To Toni. "Do you have any funny or good stories about your dad?"

> Toni: "One story Momma [Betty Ann] told me that's kinda' funny. When Daddy took her to Baltimore, they had a U haul trailer behind the car." Voice gets husky with emotion. "Momma's purse was laying on the front seat. She got out to see the woman inside about renting the place. Daddy was supposed to go around the block to line up the car so he could back it in to unload the stuff. She said he was gone a week. With her pocketbook. He got drunk."

> Toni: "I do remember there was another family that had two kids. We would play with them. One time all of us kids was playing. I was sitting there with my back to a radiator. I reared back and laughed really hard, snapping my head back. Cracked it on that radiator. I didn't know.

And one of them kids stood up behind me and said, 'Your head's bleeding!' I said 'What?' It took about eight stiches to stop the bleeding."

Me: "But where was your Daddy in that story?"

Toni: "Oh, yeah. Well, it was with these same people. They were sitting around the kitchen table and us kids were running around playing. It was three of us Russell kids and two of them. Sid hadn't been born yet. I went up to Daddy and asked for a nickel so we could go buy a pack of gum, and that way, we would each get a stick of gum." Delightedly, "Well, he gave us a quarter so we each got a pack of gum!"

Impacts and Interactions

Bill

Bill: Long pause. "I found him, you know. When he shot himself. The day he shot himself, I was twenty-five minutes behind him. Me and Agnes were looking for him. I just missed him at Payne's store. I'd just got back from my honeymoon. About a month before he done it, Dwight tried to sell me that pistol he killed himself with. Eating supper up at the house one night, and he laid that pistol up there. Said, 'Let me sell you that. Fifteen dollars.'" Pause. "I was fixin' to get married. I didn't have any money. Turned him down. When I found him, something hit me in the back. Hard. Nerves, I reckon. Dwight left a note right up there on the dash. I stuck it in my pocket before anybody seen it."

Me: "But eventually it was seen."

Bill: "No, no, no. I give it to my Momma." Long pause. "Momma gave it to Toni Ann." Long pause. "Me and

Bobby wanted to adopt the four kids after he died, when we saw how all the goings-on affected them [Agnes did too]. Betty Ann fought it. Worse than you can imagine. Toni can tell you some things. I remember Floyd Cramer's song *Last Date* was on the radio the day he died."

Susie

David (Susie's son): "The only one I never met was Dwight."

Me: "Yeah. I don't remember Dwight. Brenda does."

David: "I was born in March. And he died in…September."

Bill: "Susie was pregnant with you when he died."

David: "Yeah, Mom told those stories about him. He came by my Mom's house the night before he shot himself. Sitting out in the driveway. Mom knew he wasn't acting right. He told her, 'remember, no matter what happens…I like white roses' "There was some kind of roses in her yard that he liked."

Bill: "White roses. Susie made sure there was some white roses on his casket at the funeral."

Madge

David: "Then the next day [the day of his suicide] Dwight went by Madge's house. She saw a gun in his car. She tried to get it away from him because he was acting all weird."

Bill: "She shot his last bullet into a flower pot and give the gun back to him. But he had one more bullet she didn't know about."

Bill: "Agnes just *had* to see him dead in the car there. I tried to keep her away from the car. His '53 Olds. After that, me and her drove down to Boyd Cranford's place. Boyd was the law. We told him, he called an ambulance, and we drove back. Daddy saw us drive by at a hundred miles an hour or something, and followed us. He took charge then. When we got back home, Momma said 'Dwight's dead, isn't he?' We nodded and she grabbed her chest and had to sit down. Angina. First time she ever had angina." Grandma Lola's angina went on for the rest of her life.

Toni Ann had brought along a suitcase full of letters, files, and other items of memorabilia. Gesturing towards the suitcase. "If you want to look at any of this stuff, I brought it in."

Me: "Whatever you want to talk about, Toni. I just want to understand."

Toni: Holding out a sheaf of papers. "I've kept everything. Except his razor. I put it with my razor collection. I have a whole slew of them, and I put his in there."

Toni kept the contents of his pockets from his suicide all these years. Those contents are shown in the photo below.

Vanessa and Toni, with contents of Dwight's pockets (amid my glass case) on table in foreground (Author's photo)

Bill: Looking at Toni. "She's tough. Like Lola."

Toni: "I just did what I had to do. I wouldn't listen to Momma." Husky. "You know."

Me: "You wouldn't be controlled."

Toni: "I wouldn't be controlled."

Me: "That's why you survived and did as well as you did, you think?"

Toni: "Yes, I think so."

Toni: "So Momma said she'd never had a birthday party. My oldest girl, Sheri, was going to plan her birthday party. Well, her birthday was May 3. I showed up on May 3; no birthday party." Crying. "They had it the next day. Momma didn't want me there."

Me: "What a horrible thing. I'm so sorry."

Toni: Sobbing. "Nobody would believe me, though. Because Momma was so nice to everybody else." Sobbing. "But to me…"

Toni: "I asked her one time, I said 'Momma, I had bronchial pneumonia at eighteen months. How could you as a mother not notice a child was getting a chest infection?' She didn't answer."

Bill: "*I* know what she was doing so as not to notice her child. I tried to catch her at it. She would bundle you up real tight and go over to the Ford dealership and leave you in the back of a car, tell somebody she knew, lock the car doors, and then leave with one man or another."

Toni: "I know she made her living on her back in Baltimore."

Me: "Why did you move up there?"

Toni: "I don't know. Momma probably had a boyfriend up there."

Bill: "I remember me and Dwight drove up there to get you kids one time. Took all day to get there and all night to get home."

Toni: After a while. "It may have been partly my fault."

Me: "*No* way. No it wasn't."

Toni: "It might have been. Take a look at this bible right here. Momma give it to me a long time ago. And it was Daddy's. She sent it to him while he was in Korea. See the first page right here, this inscription. Here." I look inside. "I picked on her for spelling 'world' wrong. She put a 'u' in it." Laughs ruefully. "I said 'Momma, you spelled *world* wrong. What were you trying to spell?' So, see it might have been my fault. I was smarter at two than she was at twenty. She didn't like me for that."

Toni: "And, too, I was supposed to be a boy. When I was born. BB Dalton delivered me. When he told her I was a little girl, she cried. He said, 'You want me to put it back?' She wanted a boy."

Me: To Toni. "How old were you, when he killed himself…"

Toni: "I was six."

Toni: "Once we were driving down from Baltimore and stopped at a service station. She got back in the car and drove off. Found out I wasn't in the car about 50 miles down the road. When they come back, I was just a sittin' there with the man and the woman at the service station. I said, 'See there, she *needs* me!'"

Me: "You should be proud of your strength."

Toni: Sniffing. "I'm *not* a very strong person."

Me: Quietly. "Yes, you are. Pause. You might not feel—inside—very strong, from whatever has happened to you. But if you weren't a strong person you couldn't have survived all this."

Toni's daughter Vanessa Key

Vanessa: Looking at her mother: "This woman taught me. I've been a single mom. Never been married. Raised two kids with no child support. Bought my own home. Got two cars out in the driveway. She taught me how to balance, how to budget. Do credit. How to have things. How to be a single woman and have things. Not a lot of women know how to do that. I give all the credit to her."

Me: To Vanessa. "Do you also feel like you gave up something being like that?"

Vanessa: "Being an independent woman, you mean?"

Me: "Yes."

Vanessa: "Sometimes I do. I get lonely. Not having somebody to share my life with. I worry about dying alone. Things like that, but I don't have to put up with nobody telling me what I can and can't do, when I can do it, where I can go."

Me: "You ever meet men that appreciate that independence?"

Vanessa: Pauses. "No. I think it scares them off."

Jackie

Jackie was second. Jackie had followed in her father's footsteps and served in the Marines.

Vanessa: "Jackie is different. She has a different blood type."

Toni: "It's a p-type factor or something in her blood that's different."

Bill: "She don't look him. She don't act like him."

Me: To Toni. "Do you keep up with Jackie now?"

Toni: Flatly. "No."

Me: "She doesn't have anything to do with y'all?"

Toni: Flatly. "No."

Me: Responding to the flatness, "Do you know why?"

Toni: "Yeah, I know why. Momma had three big walk in safes, full of coins and guns and jewelry. Gold coins that Momma bought. They started disappearing before Momma died. I got wiped out of the will. I got nothing. Jackie's got everything. No, I take that back. Momma had a CD in my name. Jackie didn't know about it. $900. I got that."

Husky. Crying. "I wanted a piece of jewelry or something so I could have something to remember Momma by. Some memorable thing I'd seen her wear. You know."

Darlene

Darlene, the third child had also been a Marine.

Toni: "Darlene had a problem. I called her a 'Rock star without a guitar.' She was a crack addict when she died. She got lung cancer and it spread to her brain."

Vanessa: "I loved her. Loved her to death."

Toni: "Darlene was big hearted. She would love you, and give you anything that she had." Voice turns husky. "But she was taken advantage of. A lot. A lot. Momma treated her like a puppet. Whatever Momma wanted done, Darlene did it."

Vanessa: "She'd give you the shirt off her back. She went into the Marine Corps. She was so smart. So book smart. She read really fast, thick books in half a day. But she'd give her car away to the crack dealer on the hill for a rock, you know."

Toni: "She didn't have a lot of common sense."

Vanessa: "There is a fine line between insanity and genius. And Darlene rode…"

Toni: "Darlene rode that line, man!"

Vanessa: "I got a picture of her on my phone. She looked like Janis Joplin." Shows me the picture. There was indeed a resemblance. "She was my favorite aunt. I don't care if she had a drug problem, she was one of the most kind-hearted people. And she loved Braxton [Vanessa's son]."

Toni: "Do you remember what Braxton did at Darlene's funeral?" Knocking on table. "'Darlene, Darlene. Wake up. Welcome to Braxton's family reunion.'" Husky. "'Darlene. Get up. Come on Darlene!'"

Sid

Toni: "Sid was a big-hearted person, too. Momma told me one time—Momma always said she could see the future, that she was a white witch—and she told me one time that 'two of my kids are going to die before I die.' *He* died from a massive heart attack."

Me: "At what age?"

Toni: "Born in '58. Died in 2014. What, 56? Darlene died in 2009. And Momma died in 2016. He was bad to take just about anything anybody give him."

Vanessa: "When he got disability, he got a bunch of money. That worried me, because Uncle Sid could not control himself."

Toni: "He'd give it all away. He'd have girls at bars bend down like this and he would throw $100 bills into the middle of their boobs. How stupid can you be?"

Vanessa: "He *was* easily influenced. He did too much drugs. He didn't know when to stop. Girls would talk him into getting more, and keep getting more."

Vanessa: "He worked hard. Good with his hands. He bought a trailer. He didn't have no credit so Grandma Betty Ann got it in her name and put a lien against it. Sid probably paid for that trailer and land four times."

Toni: "Four or five times. Michael [Toni's current husband] saw Sid take ten, fourteen, thousand dollars over there and give it to her to pay off his property, to get her to sign off on the lien. She'd take it and laugh at him."

Vanessa: "Then when he died before her, it was still in her name."

●—◆—●

One particularly sad thought for me. Look below at the picture of Sid on the left and me on the right, taken at roughly the same age. Do we look a fair bit alike? I think so.

Poor Sid never had a chance. There is a lot more to Sid and the other kid's stories than what I have written here. They lived in a hell on earth.

I got what I needed and have had a happy successful marriage, career, and family life. Why? So much potential wasted with Sid. And with Dwight's other kids.

Sid (l), looking a whole lot like me (r)
(Courtesy of Toni Russell; family photo)

Summing Up

Vanessa: "Grandma Betty messed up all of y'all."

Me: To Toni. "I remember y'all when we were little. And I remember the pain that radiated off the four of you." Long pause.

Toni: As if mystified. "How could you see it?"

Me: "I don't know. I could just tell."

Toni: "But how could you tell?"

Me: "Hmmn." Long pause. "Eyes. The, the…unnatural body language. You were so still." In addition, they were wary, always watching. Hardly ever did I see one of them smile.

●◆●

Vanessa: "Just think if Dwight had gotten y'all when you was little, proving Grandma unfit, how different your life would have been."

Toni: "Yeah. I do believe my daddy was a good man. But I *know* my momma was a bad woman."

● ◆ ●

Afterwards I was talking with Bill.

Me: "The suicide note was about Betty Ann, his wife, not about PTSD or headaches."

Bill: Long look into distance. "I know."

So, I don't guess much mystery remains. I suppose it was as simple as "married too young, torn apart by war, and then down a descending spiral towards suicide over a bad woman." Bad, sad country song. I thought back to when we'd been at the graveyard at Center Church, where I had spied a small marker within grandpa and grandma's larger plot.

Me: I had nudged it, "What's this?"

Bill: "What?"

Me: "A tiny marker labelled D.R. Just D.R."

Bill: "Dwight's grave. They cremated him. They dug a hole down in there and put his urn in it."

In the marines at 17, dead at 28 of a broken heart.

According to The Asheboro Courier-Tribune newspaper, Betty Ann Lanier Russell died on March 5, 2016. No services were held.

Dwight's single act of putting a bullet into his brain resulted in so much pain for so many, and so much was never talked about. I hope this helps.

● ◆ ●

Bill: "All six of Daddy's [Cled's] boys served in the military, now."

Me: "Yes." Thoughtful pause.

Before moving along in our tour of Blaine, North Carolina, let's examine the military service records of Cled Russell's sons, and a few other folks.

CHAPTER 7

Service

Bill's Service: US Army, 1961-1963

I did not ask Bill for a copy of his service record. An oversight on my part.

>Me: "So you were in the service two years?"

>Bill: "Right."

>Me: "And they stationed you at Fort Gordon?"

>Bill: "Stewart. Fort Stewart. Did basic training at Fort Gordon in Georgia." (Fort Stewart is also in Georgia, 41 miles southwest of Savannah, and really close to Florida.)

Bill, in Army uniform (Courtesy of Bill Russell)

Me: "Ah."

Bill: "Now. You heard of the Bay of Pigs invasion?"

Me: "Oh, yeah."

Bill: "All right. Sergeant come out there one day and said to get a roll of masking tape. Now I always got a three-quarter ton truck out of the motor pool every day. I was in Range Control. They used to have a reserve firing center down there three months out of the year, and they'd come down there and use the range. Wasn't but twelve hundred people down there at Stewart. Old homesteaders place, you know. I taped up all the numbers and we went out to a field way out there to an old abandoned airfield. There sat a bunch of box trucks with no markings on 'em. Here comes some planes in. Unloaded them Cubans onto the trucks. Took 'em out into the impact area, and I went out there and put up road blocks."

Me: Incredulous. "Did you know who they were when they got off the plane?"

Bill: "I wasn't supposed to." Laughter. "I didn't have no secret clearance."

Me: "You put two and two together."

Bill: "I knew what was going on." Pause. "They took 'em out there into the impact area and trained them. In the impact area now, can't nobody get in there 'cause there's duds laying in there. Artillery shoots in there, you know. I put up signs, roadblocks. 'Keep out,' and stuff. They trained 'em for six or eight weeks, took 'em down to Cuba and they was all killed. Got 'em from Miami and flew them up there. They was volunteers."

Me: "They thought they were going to take their country back."

Bill: "Yep." Pause.

•◆•

Bill: "There was a boy in there one day, he had been a journalist. Been in there six months. He was talking to his Momma somewhere up in New Jersey and told her 'Well, I don't think this is going to amount to much.' He hadn't got more than fifty feet from that phone booth till two guys grabbed him and got him to the side. They'd had the phones tapped. Everything was tapped down there. They hauled him off to the orderly room, where he stayed for two to three weeks. They kept him in there until his background was checked out. And his people's backgrounds."

Me: "Kind of stupid on his part."

Bill: "Yeah. But they always told us if you go into town, don't you never tell nothing about what was going on over there at that base. You better not say something, 'cause you didn't know who you was talking to. Get your ass in trouble." Pause.

•◆•

Bill: "First Armored Division was right there. 28,000 men. Combat ready. Waitin' to see what they did out in the water. Boy, they was ready."

Me: "B-47s and B-52's were loaded and ready to go."

Bill: "Lot of activity down on that base when that was going on. Tanks were moving. All the equipment."

Me: Holding two fingers up close together. "I think it was just about that close. Don't you?"

Bill: Contemplative. "Could have. Could have. But these boys was ready to go to Savannah for embarkation, before you could go to Cuba. That's where they was goin'." Pause. "It was funny to go to bed in there in the night and know that you might wake up in the morning in a full scale war just 90 mile off the coast." Pause. "But you're ready. They prepare you. Prepare you to kill." Pause. "The embarkation point was somewhere in Florida. Them boys went down there to Cuba and got killed. After it was all over, Kennedy flew down. All 28,000 men who had been ready to invade Cuba was brought out onto the parade grounds. They drove Kennedy out there in a '61 Ford. Kennedy thanked all the soldiers."

Me: "You get close to him, or just from a distance?"

Bill: Pointing at a wall about twenty feet away, "Closer than that wall there."

Me: "What was he like?"

Bill: "Well, he was all over the equipment, looking at it."

Me: "Yeah, he was in World War II."

Bill: "Right. He walked fast. Real fast. A little guy, not all that big."

Bill: "Then it was over. I was told it all cost the taxpayer one million dollars."

Bill: "We had training movies, about the Second World War? And the atomic bomb. Training films. Boy, now you talk about something powerful. Take a building like this and blow it away."

Me: "They didn't know what it was going to do."

Bill: "Melt the skin off people."

David: "Yeah. And what's bad is that compared to what we have now those bombs were small. One missile might have 100 now. What's scary is so many people are threatened."

Bill: "Dwight died in '60. The Army got me away from here, and I'm glad they did. Got me in '61."

Me: "It's good we didn't attack Cuba. Might have been the end."

Bill: "Al Downing, pitched for the New York Yankees?"

Me: "Yeah?"

Bill: "I was in the service with him. They were doing a six month tour. He was on his way from New York to Florida for Spring Training. Stopped there and did his three months. I tried to get him to pitch, play with us. But that sucker, he wouldn't touch a baseball. He would not touch a baseball while he was in camp."

Justin: "He was under contract, I reckon. He hurt his arm, it'd cost him."

Bill: "Steve Spurrier. I was in there with him, too."

Me: "Seriously?"

Bill: "Serious as a heart attack. Slept in the same barracks with him."

Me: "Wow. Steve Spurrier and Al Downing."

Bill: "Yeah. Al Downing was black. Good pitcher."

Me: "You talk to Spurrier?"

Bill: "Oh, yeah."

Me: "What was he like?"

Bill: "Back then?"

Me: "Yeah."

Bill: "He was just one of 'you.'"

Eugene's Service:

Eugene, served in the Merchant Marines. He sailed into Russia, into Murmansk, as well as several other places. He gave me several coins from overseas, including two Russian pieces. The Army had ruled him 4F for flat feet, he got his 1A right after the war ended.

That is all I was able to find out about Eugene's service. His surviving family were not available to talk with me.

Homer's Service-US Army, 1944-1946, Philippines and Japan. Invasion force

Decorations and Medals: Asiatic Pacific Service Medal, Good Conduct Medal, World War II Victory Medal, Occupation Medal.

A review of Homer's service record shows that his date of entry was 5 December 1944 and date of discharge was 1 December 1946. He was a graduate of the Parachute School, and was qualified as a Rifleman. He left service as a Tec 5 Heavy Truck Driver (931). He served overseas a total of 1 year and 1 month. He received an honorable discharge.

Homer (l), with John Leonard
(Family photo)

David, to me: "Now, your daddy. Didn't he go into Japan after the war?"

Bill: "He jumped in there the day the war ended."

Me: "I never heard he did *that*. Always told me he was on a transport ship when the bomb was dropped."

Bill: "He jumped the day the war ended. Paratroopers."

David: "What part of Japan was he in?"

David: "Anywhere near Hiroshima?"

Me: "No, nothing like that. He was in the invasion force, but they got diverted to the Philippines. On a landing ship when the 1st atomic bomb was dropped and at sea when the 2nd was dropped. Went to base on the Kwajalein atoll. There were ships everywhere."

Bill: "They jumped into Japan."

Me: "Did they? He told you that?"

Bill: "Yeah. The day the war ended."

Me: "Well, he brought back some interesting pictures from over there."

Me: "They had them shoot when Dad was in basic. M1 rifle from a thousand yards. First shot was a bullseye. Then he realized what that meant." Pause. "He didn't want to be a sniper. He became a paratrooper."

David: "Being a paratrooper is pretty cool, though."

Me: "Yep. Some of the training, like jumping from 500 feet, which was so low that a reserve chute couldn't deploy. Or the time they tested some sort of new camouflage chute made out of rayon or some other synthetic material. Normally chutes were made of silk. Didn't deploy. Just about the time he was going to pull his reserve chute, the primary deployed. He looked up at it and saw all sorts of tears in it. Guess the material needed some work."

Me: "I think it hurt his back." Pause. "Told me they gave them all a case of beer a week on the beach in the Philippines. He hauled Japanese bodies out of the hills there."

David: "Whoa."

Homer Proudly Wearing the Uniform! (Family photo)

John Leonard's Service, US Army, Austria

I was unable to contact anyone in John Leonard's family to discuss his service record.

Bill: "Anybody ever tell you about John Leonard getting whipped in service?"

Me: "Nope."

Bill: "He had stripes across his back to the day he died. Whipped. Somebody beat him."

Me: "Was it because of the girl he got pregnant over there?

Bill: "No. No. He just got in the wrong crowd over there. I figured he just got in the wrong place." Pause. "Maybe the enemy or something. He never did tell nobody about that. Madge seen him one time with his shirt off."

Me: "Strange."

Bill: "I know it. But John Leonard, he didn't talk. Somewhere over there he has a daughter he never saw."

Loy's Service (Agnes' husband) 1944-1946, US Army, Normandy invasion force

Decorations and Medals: American Theater Ribbon, EAMLT Campaign Ribbon with 3 Bronze Service Stars, and a Victory medal.

Loy Dennis (Courtesy of John Russell)

David: "I never realized that Mutt [Agnes' husband Loy Dennis] went into St Lo. Right inside Normandy."

The Battle for St. Lo

The Battle for St. Lo occurred over a six-week period soon after the Normandy invasion. The bocage territory around St. Lo--15 foot high hedgerows--was extremely effective for German defensive positions. St. Lo was called "The Capital of Ruins," and was very strategically located. It was the first city liberated by the Allies from Germans.

The battle for St. Lo has been called the bloodiest battle of the war. 95% of the city was destroyed in the fighting. Casualties were 60% of enlisted men and 68% of the officers between June 6 and July 31, 1944, with 90% losses within the rifle platoons.

While the Allies did not meet all of their geographical goals, they did severely reduce the German's ability to wage effective war going forward.

Me: "Surrounded, right?"

Justin: "They was fightin' room to room. One of the most brutal battles."

Thomas Bonner, recollection from talking with Homer: "Loy went into Omaha beach a few days after D-Day, then went across the bocage, the hedgerow land. He was a heavy machine gunner. His unit was isolated for two days at St. Lo. Many of his buddies were killed and injured."

Me: "And he survived it."

David: "Yep. He got shell shocked. He got medals out of that."

Bill: "But when you was around Mutt, you never knew it. If anybody saw that Purple Heart he had, he would say, 'I got that off an old boy I knew.'" (Briden Russell was killed in the Philippines and reportedly got a Purple Heart. Maybe Loy had Briden's Purple Heart. Loy's record does not show a Purple Heart.)

Me: "Right. Wow. But he was…detached."

Bill: "Right."

David: "He didn't like to talk."

Me: "He was a nice guy." Pause. "I guess after that, pretty much anything would be a nice life, huh?

General agreement.

David: "I told my boys one day, 'You go through something like that, and nothing else ever seems very important.'"

Justin: "I remember when I was a kid, and we'd go visit. He was always really nice."

David, reflectively: "Yeah, but you know he always had a gun out. We would walk in with the kids, and he would grab that gun and put it up."

Me: "I did not know that."

David: "Oh, yeah."

Me: "He never talked about the war."

David: "Naw, not much. One day we got to talking, I mean, with the boys. They was old enough to talk. We were at the hospital visiting somebody and he said, 'Come down to the house sometime, and I'll tell you about it.' And I *never* did. I just *hate* that."

John: "Loy wouldn't drink warm water. And he wouldn't eat spaghetti or pizza. From his war experiences, I reckon. You know."

John: "He was in the 29th Infantry Division. Saw the Rhineland, St. Lo. Started in the infantry. Then became a MP. In the infantry."

Justin: "Took a different kind of man to do that stuff."

Me: "The last good war."

Dwight's service. 3 tours US Marine Corp, 1952-1960. Served in Korean War.

Decorations and Medals: Korean Service Medal, United Nations Service Medal, Korean Presidential Unit Citation, Good Conduct Medal.

A review of Dwight's service record shows that he had three tours of duty. His date of entry was 15 February 1952 and date of discharge was 6 May 1960. He attended Leadership training. He left service as an E-3 Auto Mechanic 3516. He served overseas a total of 2 years and 12 days. He was discharged under honorable conditions.

Devereaux's service. US Army, 1959-1961, Germany, 1st How Bn 35th Arty.

Devereaux in Germany (Courtesy of John Russell)

I did not ask to see Devereaux's service record. An oversight on my part.

> Virginia: "Devereaux didn't drink or smoke. In the military, he liked to say he was a loan-shark. That's what we would call him. Everybody got cigarettes and Devereaux would sell his towards the end of the month. Charged them interest. Like a loan shark. Then, when John was in

service [Gulf War, US Army] he did the same thing, but he would demand collateral."

John: "Right. If they didn't pay me back, I kept the collateral. Although the boys in my unit knew I liked those dehydrated strawberries that came along in the MREs every once in a while. They'd trade them every time for my cigs."

Others in WW II

Sgt. Briden Russell, died in Philippines, 3/16/1945 (Courtesy of John Russell)

American War of Independence

West Harris, Sr. served in the American Revolution at age 69, holding rank of Major.

West Harris Senior's son, Colonel West Harris—as he was always referred to in my hearing (not as William West Harris, Jr)—entered the North Carolina Line of the Continental Army as a Lieutenant at a very young age. He was in the Battles of Brandywine, Kings Mountain, Guilford Courthouse, and spent the winter at Valley

Forge, Pennsylvania. He was at Yorktown when General Cornwallis surrendered. In his application for pension of 16 April 1834, a Joshua Hurley spoke of a march to Wilmington, North Carolina, with Major West Harris, Captain Etheldred Harris, and others to protect that port after the departure of Lord Cornwallis on 25 April 1781. West was later promoted to the rank of Colonel.

Captain Etheldred Harris, West's brother, was in the North Carolina State Militia.

Serving the Confederacy

After North Carolina seceded on May 20, 1861, Zebedee Russell dutifully served in the Confederate Army as a Captain, and was pardoned by President Andrew Johnson in 1866, as shown below.

376

ANDREW JOHNSON,

PRESIDENT OF THE UNITED STATES OF AMERICA,

To all to whom these presents shall come, Greeting:

Whereas, Zebedee Russell ...

And whereas, ...

Now, therefore, be it known, that I, ANDREW JOHNSON, President of the United States ...

In testimony whereof, ...

By the President:

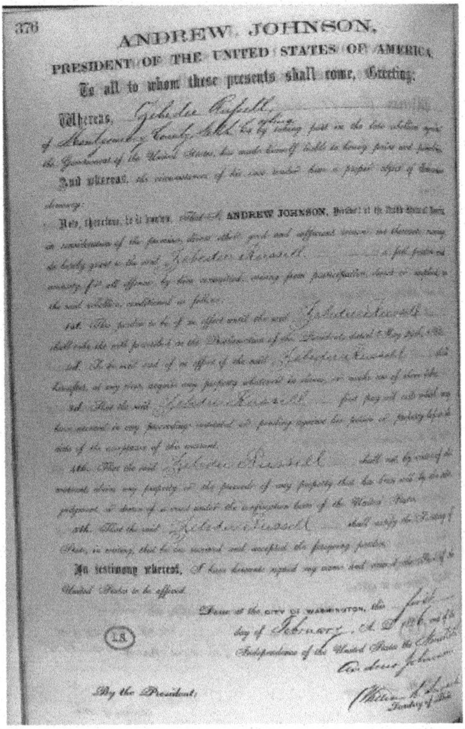

Zebedee Russell's Presidential Pardon (Ancestry.com)

In *Montgomery County Heritage-Volume III*, J.W. Houston quotes General James Longstreet: "I have found more dead North Carolinean's on battlefields of Virginia than any other state," and that "25% of the casulties from the battle of Gettysburg were from North Carolina." Zeb and other North Carolinians, did the duty they were assigned for North Carolina.

Atlas Russell, Zeb's son, enlisted as a Private in Company K, 14th Infantry Regiment North Carolina on 21 May 1861. He died of disease as a POW on 12 Oct 1862 at Old Capitol Prison, Washington D.C. Other reports state that he died at Gettysburg on July 1, 1863.

Gilbert Russell (3rd generation great uncle) died in a Civil War POW camp at Point Lookout, MD in 1865.

50 Caliber Bullets from unknown Russells during Civil War (Courtesy of John Russell)

CHAPTER 8

From the Slave Graveyard to Low Water Bridge and Back to Where We Started

Bill drives the short distance to the Coggins Mine Road and turns right. Less than a mile down on the left is the Low Water Bridge Road. We turn. It is a mile to the Low Water Bridge itself.

Bill, pointing out the window of his truck. "This down here is where Cicero Hurley lived. Called him Bigfoot. And they used to hide liquor under that bridge right there. Call it Low Water Bridge. Kids found ten cases of liquor one time. Moonshine. You never been to the Low Water Bridge?"

Me: "No."

Bill: "We used to come down here on Sunday evening and play. Get out of church and eat dinner."

Bill: "This is where Devereaux come over one Saturday night. Been over here across the river to see a girl. And the river was flooding. Over the bridge? And I come across down through there about 12:30 on Saturday night. Cold. Rainy. And I seen some tail lights setting down there at the river. And it was Devereaux. '49 Pontiac. He couldn't back up the hill and he couldn't go forwards." Pause. "We tried for a while, then I said, 'Listen here, let some air out of your tires. Get some traction.' He did, and backed right out of there."

Bill, pointing out towards a flat area near the water: "Now. Another time. Two cars pulled up in there. This Captain Lanier from the State Highway Patrol told Mutt [Agnes' husband Loy Dennis] about it down at the store. There was nothing built up in here like it is now. Captain Lanier was laying up here on the ridge watching. So the two cars come in. They pulled right in there. It was just an old turn around. The captain put his binoculars on them. Two men got out. Two cars. They got a suitcase out. Opened it up. Full of money. I'm talking about this was years-s-s-s ago. Long time ago." Pause.

Bill: "Lots of people kayaks down through there now. This bridge crosses the Uwharrie River." Looks into the distance down the river.

We pile back in Bill's truck and head back to Coggins Mine Road. We turn left. We drive by the entrance to the Coggins Mine, which is a quarter mile or less away.

Coggins Mine

Bill: "This is the old Coggins Mine we're going past. Old mine was right here on the left." Pointing. "And that's the old mine office right there. Miners used to live there."

Me: "Miners or the superintendent?"

Bill: "Miners. All this was the mine's property."

Bill: "Now. You got that thing [my recorder] on?" I nod. "Beecher Holt lived there at the old Coggins mine. Had some ducks. He sold one to a man in Uwharrie. And the man killed it, and cut its craw open. It was full of gold nuggets." Pause. "Beecher said he'd never 'sell another damn duck' till he weighed it!" Cackle.

Me: "Wow!"

Bill: "Duck's eat anything that's laying around. You know." Pause. Pointing. "Ralph Holt lived there. He showed me one time a little 'baccer [tobacco] sash. Just full of nuggets he'd found around there." Pointing down a side road. "Ken Holt lived down there. I cut my foot in his pond on an old broke liquor bottle."

The Coggins Mine was operated on and off from 1882 to 1934. The Coggins Mine was something that *was* talked about within the extended family. As mentioned earlier, neither my sister nor I had ever heard about the Russell Gold Mine. Of course, the Coggins Mine had been worked more recently.

And there were a lot of stories related to the Coggins Mine that Uncle Bill and his siblings heard from people then living. Grandpa Cled actually worked there, and Grandma Lola took care of Great-grandma Corilla's boarders, who themselves worked in the mine.

Harvey Younts, a Thomasville native and retired Wal-Mart employee, has spent the past thirty-seven years mining or panning for gold in the Uwharrie Mountains of Montgomery County. Ten years ago, Younts purchased the site of the old Coggins Mine.

After roughly a mile or slightly more, we turn right onto Highway 109. We're just past the turn onto Highway 109.

Bill: "See where the pines are? The ball field. That's where we used to play church league softball. Growed up all to weeds now." Pause. "I'll show you a picture of the team after we get home." Laugh.

Front row, from left: Vance Coggins, Bill Clark, Frank Coggins, Ed Davis, Jack Morris

Back row, from left: Charles Clark, Clayton Cobb, Jerry Thompson, Beecher Holt, Devereaux Russell (Courtesy of Bill Russell)

Bill: "I had gone to the beach the week when they made that picture. I wasn't in it. I'll tell you something. That Devereaux could slap a damn ball. Hit one down there one night to dead center. There was a '50 Mercury sitting out there. Went right through the windshield."

Bill: "Devereaux could really hit it. He played third base. I played shortstop. As the youngest, when we first started playing I was hardly big enough to play. I remember once going up to bat and swinging as hard as I could at a pitch, hitting it, and being spun around by the ball on the bat."

Me: "Dwight would pitch?"

Bill: "Oh, no. He didn't play with us. This was '55, '56. Church league. For the Fourth of July game, the rest of the league picked up the best players from other teams, then went to Winston and picked up a semi-pro pitcher and his catcher, 'cause he was so fast couldn't nobody else catch him. Give him $40 and all the liquor he could drink, I think. They were so tired of losing to us."

Me: "To play your team?"

Bill: "Yep. An all-star team from all the other teams. We was the first ball team in Montgomery County to light a ball field. High school didn't even have it."

Me: "Why were y'all better? Weren't they all country boys, too?"

Bill: "Naw. They normally got the high school boys from down there at Troy. City boys. Couldn't beat us." Pause. "If we weren't playing every night, we was practicin'. Had lights; didn't none of the rest of 'em have lights. We'd cut the pole, have a christening, and put it in the ground, run lights around there. Fourth of July weekend, there were a hundred cars lined up around that field. I bet there was 300 people there watching that game." Pause. "We won the championship two years straight."

Me: "Sounds great."

Bill: "Couldn't nobody beat us. We won every game in 1955 and 1956."

Virginia: "At Devereaux's visitation, a man came up to me, told me Devereaux was the best player he ever saw. 'If not for his knees,' the man said, 'he could probably have played pro ball.'"

Me, to Bill: "Dad [Homer] coached our church league team three years, did you know that?"

1966 team photo
Homer (l, back row)

Bill: "Heard something about that."

Me: "It was the worst team in the league when [1966] he started coaching it. The last year, he didn't lose a game."

Bill: "Really," as if mildly surprised. "I told you we was determined."

Me: Laughing. "Yeah. He always played right field in our neighborhood games. We used the backyards of two next door neighbors for our field. He didn't have sneakers, would play out there in his black work shoes. Never missed a fly ball, no grounders ever got through. I always thought he just loved playing the game. It was many years later before I realized that by playing right field he was guarding his house and windows from stray balls." Laugh.

Me: Pause. "He was a good coach. To me and a lot of other people. And he *was* determined."

We are now somewhere past the location of the old ball field.

Bill: "Old 109 highway used to come through there. Right yonder. I'll show you in a minute. Oops, can't get through there. That road don't go through no more. But, see that tree, that tall tree there? There was a spring over there. And that's where the tan yard used to be."

Me: "It was owned by…Grandma's dad?"

Bill: "Yeah. My Momma's daddy. Glen Harris. That's all I know about it."

Me: Who would know about it?"

Bill: "Grey Harris would know, but he's not too clear headed. Uh, Robert's dead. Tell you the truth, I don't really know."

So I investigated the tannery. Here's what I found out:

Per a *Montgomery Herald* article from June 3, 1992, "The community of Eldorado, long before gold was discovered there, was known as 'Tan Yard.'"

Leonard Harris was the tanner at one time. One day he had been tanning, and stopped to go into a store. Tanning was very dirty and he had on a long apron over his normal clothes. Leonard was known to be a kind man. The salesman in the store looked at him and said, "You are probably the dirtiest man I've ever seen." Leonard replied, "It's all on the outside—just on the outside."

Finally, NM Thayer was the area tanner in 1889, as he was listed thusly in the year's listing of area businesses. I still don't know exactly where the tannery was.

We drive a mile along Highway 109, and pull up in front of what the family always called the Eldorado House.

Front of house in Eldorado
(Author's photo)

Bill: "Daddy bought the house at Eldorado from Aunt Ethel ['Ma's' sister]. There was two girls, Ethel and Ma. Ma died. It was her house, and was Ma's base for her mid-wifing. Daddy bought Aunt Ethel's part. He remodeled it with timber off his land. John Leonard helped him. That's one of the oldest houses in Montgomery County. No nails holding them. Notched and lapped. Pegged. Big 'ol pegs. Used a foot adze. There's boards in there, 23 inches wide. No knots, nothing. And I told you Ma used to keep boarders there."

Me: "Yes. I liked that old house. Hot in the summer, though."

We walk behind the house.

Bill: "Yeah. Rottin' down now, though." Pause. "That old black oak was back here. They used to water horses right there."

Me: "And the outhouse was back there."

Bill: "Yep. It burnt down." Pause. Pointing at a garage separate from the house. "Daddy and Devereaux built that right there."

Going into house via the side door

Me: "Used to be a black cherry here. [Near the side door]."

David: "Used to be a spigot right there. And they had that little ladle hanging in the tree right there." Pause. To Bill. "Me and Doug used to play king of the hill down there," pointing down the hill in front of the house.

Me: "We sure did."

David: "Throw the football. That's when I started liking the Dallas Cowboys. Doug liked the Redskins, so I had to always be the Cowboys. It's Doug's fault I like the Cowboys!"

Me, woeful little shake of my head.

Inside the house.

Bill: "Up there [second floor bedroom] is where Daddy—He wasn't in his mind no more—almost burned the house down. You can see the scorched floor. He left a heater on. House would have burned down if Lola hadn't gone up there" Pause. "He didn't have sense to know it. He had Alzheimer's. He had hardening of the arteries. And me and Dwight slept up there after he moved in for a while when Dwight was separated, like we talked about."

We get into Bill's truck and headed up Highway 109 back to the Center United Methodist Church, where my car is parked. Along the way, Uncle Bill points out the window at a patch of non-descript woods. "Over there is where Dwight killed himself."

I say nothing. There is nothing more to say.

The tour of Blaine is over.

As Devereaux's son, John Russell said, "We got it all. What a family! Stories about gold, cheatin', drugs, land, sex, crazies, war, and whatever else you can find in a good old country song!"

Bill and several of them became quite well off, mainly from hard work in industrial machine maintenance, wood carving, and furniture making. The detail in the stories Bill relayed across so many years was incredible. I should hope to do so well when I'm eighty.

While it was obvious from looking around that nothing much seems to be going on in the Blaine area now, it and the people in Blaine came alive in his stories. I had no idea the Russell family had been distinguished at one time. State delegates, founding members of the county capital, owners of broad swathes of land and a gold mine, they became dirt poor, first from the Civil War, and then when the Depression hit hard during the 1930s.

When the mines closed, jobs and people left for Asheboro, Greensboro, Troy, and elsewhere. Somewhere along the way, the Russells from Blaine lost their collective memories about owning gold mines and five-hundred acre sections of land. Uncle Bill provided the impetus to help me discover those things.

Yep. Just a bit of "every-day living." And it was all *real*.

ACKNOWLEDGEMENTS

I want to thank Uncle Bill from the bottom of my heart. There would be no book without his suggestion that "you boys need to hear about the old times."

Nothing good in my life would be possible without the support of my wonderful wife, Anne Trent Russell. Her superb editing overcame my rushing ways. Any errors that remain are mine.

Thanks to John Russell, Devereaux's son. Much of the Russell family archive of data resides with John. Early on in the research for this book, he said, "You can look at anything I got, Doug." And he had a lot!

Thanks to my sister Brenda Russell Bonner for answering *so* many questions, for several stories and photos, and for a copy of the Land Grant.

Thanks to the folks who patiently let me interview them, including Aunts Virginia Russell and Bobbie Russell, David Rothrock, his sons Justin and Jordan, Toni Russell, Vanessa Key, Thomas Bonner, Kathy Russell, Carlene Coggins, and Jennie Russell Clark.

Thanks to Guy Hall and his team at the Atlanta Archives; to Matthew Dibiase and his team at the Philly Archives; to Ellen Show at the Charlotte Mint Museum; to Lauren Murphee and her colleagues at the State Archive of North Carolina-Raleigh.

Fisher Family papers staff at Wilson Library, University of North Carolina at Chapel Hill

Special Collection staff at JY Joyner Library, East Carolina University.

BIBLIOGRAPHY

Research papers:

Chapter 2, *The Carolina Slate Belt*, www.rla.unc.edu, John JW Rogers. *Harris* and. *Glover 1988*; *Rogers 1999*

Williams, R.S., Jr., and Kover, A.N., 1978, Remote sensing: *Geotimes*, v. 23, no. 1.

FUSGS Remote Sensing in the USGS Mineral Resource Surveys Program in the Eastern United States https://pubs.usgs.gov/info/rowan_Klein, Terry; Cunningham, Charles; Logan, M.A.V.

Seal II, Robert R., *"The Russell Gold Deposit, Carolina Slate Belt, North Carolina" (2007)*. USGS Staff — Published Research.

Foley, N.K., and Ayuso, R.A., 2012, *Gold deposits of the Carolina Slate Belt, southeastern United States—Age and origin of the major gold producers*: U.S. Geological Survey Open-File Report 2012–1179

North Carolina Geological Survey, J. A. Holmes, State Geologist, Bulletin No. 3 Gold Deposits of North Carolina, by Henry B.C. Nitze and George B. Hanna, 1896.

Principal Gold-Producing Districts of the United States By A. H. Koschmann and M. H. Bergendahl Geological Survey Professional Paper 610 United States Government Printing Office, Washington 1968.

The Rush Started Here II: Hard Rock Gold Mining In North Carolina, 1825 TO 1864, Elizabeth Hines and Michael Smith, Department of Earth Sciences, University of North Carolina, U.S.A.

1853 Report of the Perseverance Mining Company (Philip T. Tyson) w/ Map (North Carolina), John Toy, Baltimore, MD, 1853.

Books:

Barfield, Rodney and Keith Strawn. *The Bechtlers and Their Coins.* North Carolina Museum of History, 1980.

Bynum, Victoria E. *Unruly Women: the Politics of Social and Sexual Control in the Old South.* Univ. of North Carolina Press, 1992.

Latta, Estelle. *Controversial Mark Hopkins.* Cothran Historical and Research Foundation, 1963.

Montgomery County Historical Society, *Montgomery County Heritage-North Carolina Vol I and Vol III,* Delmar Printing, 1992 and 2001.

Naugle, June. *The Great American Swindle.* Author House, 2007.

Ramirez, Salvador A. *The Inside Man: the Life and Times of Mark Hopkins of New York, Michigan, and California.* Tentacled Press, 2007.

Rayner, Richard. *The Associates: Four Capitalists Who Created California.* W Norton, 2009.

Redding, Benjamin B. *A Sketch of the Life of Mark Hopkins.* Forgotten Books, 2015.

Vance, J. D. *Hillbilly Elegy: a Memoir.* Harper, an Imprint of HarperCollinsPublishers, 2016.

Winter, Douglas. *Charlotte Mint Gold Coins, 1838-1861: a Numismatic History and Analysis.* Bowers and Merena Galleries, 1987.

Zaloga, Steven J. *St Lo 1944: The Battle of the Hedgerows*. Osprey Publishing, 2017.

Articles:

"Gold Mining in the Uwharries," by Kenneth W. Robinson, published in the Fall 2008 by the Tar Heel Junior Historical Association

Pine Straw magazine: https://www.pinestrawmag.com/gold-rush/. Bill Fields. March 2017 issue "Gold Rush."

Our State, ourstate.com/north-carolina-gold-rush/

New York Sun newspaper, "The Gold Fields of North Carolina." North Carolina Gold Mining and Bullion Co., June 7, 1891.

Internet:

Army Study Guide, armystudyguide.com.

Dependent Personality Disorder, www.psychologytoday.com/us/conditions/.

Diana, Goddess of the Hunt Genealogy Website: dgmweb.net/FGS/H/HopkinsMark-MaryFrancesSherwood

Gold Fever and the Bechtler Mint: The Bechtler Story, goldfever.unctv.org

1910 Map of Eldorado Township, www.censusfinder.com

NC Manual 1913, carolana.com

www.familysearch.org

Gold History & Mining: eldoradooutpost.com

Montgomery Register of Deeds (montgomeryrod.net)

Wells Fargo v Estelle Latta: caselaw.findlaw.com/ca-court-of-appeal/1822505.html

https://www.newspapers.com/US/North Carolina/Raleigh/News and Observer_3272

www.nclandgrants.com/

SEC v. LATTA case: http://ca.findacase.com/research/wfrm-DocViewer.aspx/xq/fac.19650426_0000017.NCA.htm/qx

www.ncpedia.org/biography/fisher-charles-frederick

courier-tribune.com (Betty Ann obit)

www.renegadesouth.wordpress.com/2009/06/19/the-inner-civil-war-in-montgomery-co-n-c/

www.webgis.net/nc/Montgomery/

Find A Grave, database and images (https://www.findagrave.com : accessed 03 September 2018), memorial page for Capt. Zebedee Russell (19 Apr 1805–19 Mar 1886), Find A Grave Memorial no. 42935879, citing Russell Cemetery, Montgomery County, North Carolina, USA ;Maintained by Donnie Ruyle (contributor 46921690)

northcarolina.hometownlocator.com

Ross Winans, "A Communication to the President and Directors of the B&O RR Co. on the Subject of Locomotive Engines for Transporting Freight on Railroads," (Baltimore: John D. Toy, 1856), B&O Railroad Company archives. www.borail.org.

www.digitalhistory.uh.edu

www.wikipedia.com

www.dc.lib.unc.edu

www.ancestry.com